LET'S LEARN
ITALIAN
PICTURE DICTIONARY

By
The Editors of
Passport Books

Illustrated by
Marlene Goodman

McGraw·Hill

New York   Chicago   San Francisco   Lisbon   London   Madrid   Mexico City
Milan   New Delhi   San Juan   Seoul   Singapore   Sydney   Toronto

Welcome to the *Let's Learn Italian* Picture Dictionary!

Here's an exciting way for you to learn more than 1,500 Italian words that will help you speak about many of your favorite subjects. With these words, you will be able to talk in Italian about your house, sports, outer space, the ocean, and many more subjects.

This dictionary is fun to use. On each page, you will see drawings with the Italian and English words that describe them underneath. These drawings are usually part of a large, colorful scene. See if you can find all the words in the big scene and then try to remember how to say each one in Italian. You will enjoy looking at the pictures more and more as you learn more Italian.

You will notice that almost all the Italian words in this book have **il, lo, l', gli, la,** or **le** before them. These words simply mean "the"

and are usually used when you talk about things in Italian.

At the back of the book, you will find an Italian-English Glossary and Index and an English-Italian Glossary and Index, where you can look up words in alphabetical order, and find out exactly where the words are located in the dictionary. There is also a section that explains how you say Italian sounds as well as pronunciation guides that will help you say each Italian word correctly.

This is a book you can look at over and over again, and each time you look, you will find something new. You'll learn the Italian words for people, places, and things you know, and you may even learn some new words in English as you go along!

The McGraw·Hill Companies

Library of Congress Cataloging-in-Publication Data

Let's learn Italian picture dictionary / by the editors of Passport Books ; illustrated by Marlene Goodman.
    1 v. (unpaged) : col. Ill., col. Map ; 31 cm
    Includes indexes.
    ISBN 0-07-140826-6 (alk. paper)
    1. Italian language—Dictionaries, Juvenile—English.
  2. English language—Dictionaries, Juvenile—Italian.
  3. Picture dictionaries, Italian—Juvenile literature.
  4. Picture dictionaries, English—Juvenile literature.
  5. Picture dictionaries, Italian.   6. Picture dictionaries.
  7. Italian language materials—Bilingual.

PC1640 .L398   2002
453'.21—dc20   2003265133

Illustrations by Terrie Meider
7. Clothing; 15. People in Our Community; 18. Sports; 28. Colors; 29. The Family Tree; 30. Shapes; 31. Numbers; 32. Map of the World

14 15 16 17 18 19   WKT/WKT 14 13

ISBN 0-07-140826-6

McGraw-Hill books are available at special quantity discounts to use as premiums and sales promotions, or for use in corporate training programs. For more information, please write to the Director of Special Sales, Professional Publishing, McGraw-Hill, Two Penn Plaza, New York, NY 10121-2298. Or contact your local bookstore.

This book is printed on acid-free paper.

Table of Contents
Indice

1. Our Classroom Nostra Classe

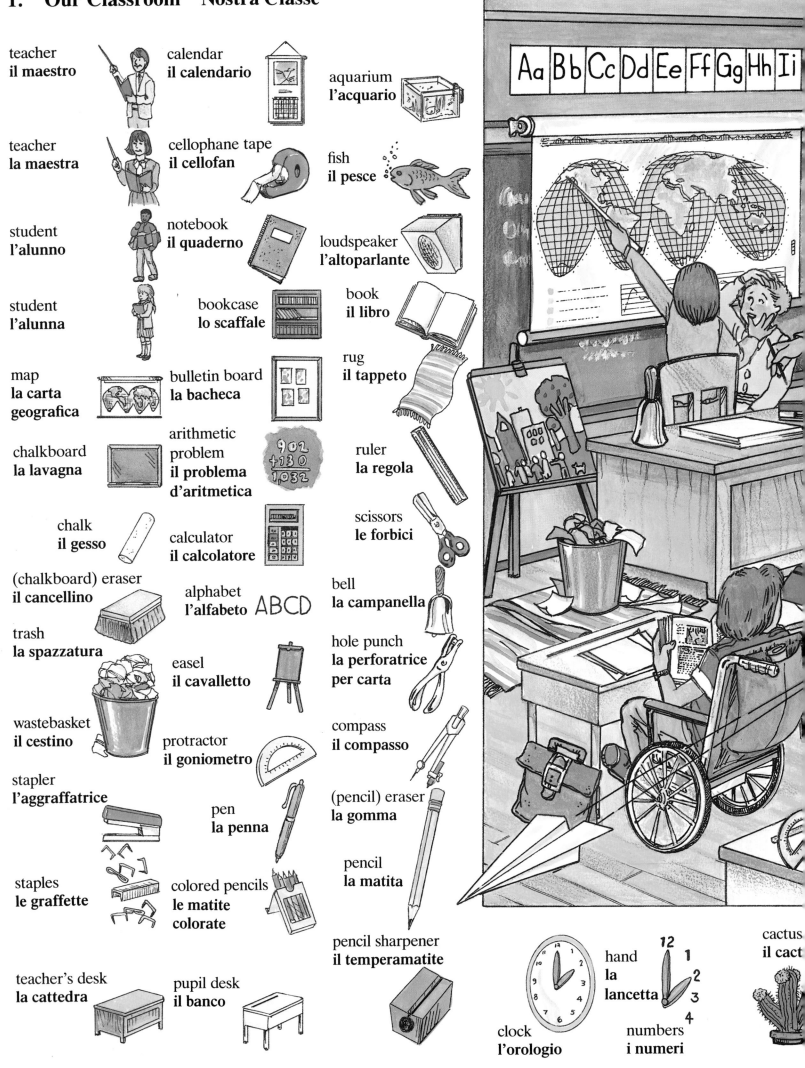

teacher
il maestro

calendar
il calendario

aquarium
l'acquario

teacher
la maestra

cellophane tape
il cellofan

fish
il pesce

student
l'alunno

notebook
il quaderno

loudspeaker
l'altoparlante

student
l'alunna

bookcase
lo scaffale

book
il libro

map
la carta geografica

bulletin board
la bacheca

rug
il tappeto

chalkboard
la lavagna

arithmetic problem
il problema d'aritmetica

ruler
la regola

chalk
il gesso

calculator
il calcolatore

scissors
le forbici

(chalkboard) eraser
il cancellino

alphabet
l'alfabeto ABCD

bell
la campanella

trash
la spazzatura

easel
il cavalletto

hole punch
la perforatrice per carta

wastebasket
il cestino

protractor
il goniometro

compass
il compasso

stapler
l'aggraffatrice

pen
la penna

(pencil) eraser
la gomma

staples
le graffette

colored pencils
le matite colorate

pencil
la matita

pencil sharpener
il temperamatite

teacher's desk
la cattedra

pupil desk
il banco

clock
l'orologio

hand
la lancetta

numbers
i numeri

cactus
il cact[us]

plant
la pianta

glue
la colla

globe
il globo

picture
il quadro

paint
il colore

paintbrush
il pennello

paper
la carta

crayon
il pastello

2. Our House
La Nostra Casa

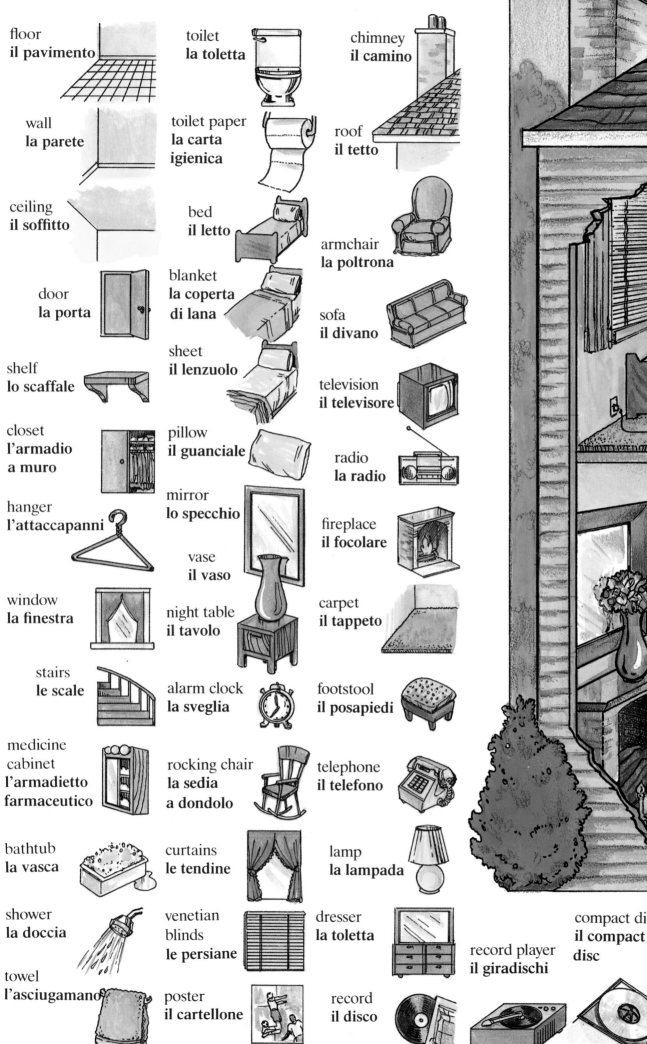

floor
il pavimento

wall
la parete

ceiling
il soffitto

door
la porta

shelf
lo scaffale

closet
**l'armadio
a muro**

hanger
l'attaccapanni

window
la finestra

stairs
le scale

medicine
cabinet
**l'armadietto
farmaceutico**

bathtub
la vasca

shower
la doccia

towel
l'asciugamano

toilet
la toletta

toilet paper
**la carta
igienica**

bed
il letto

blanket
**la coperta
di lana**

sheet
il lenzuolo

pillow
il guanciale

mirror
lo specchio

vase
il vaso

night table
il tavolo

alarm clock
la sveglia

rocking chair
**la sedia
a dondolo**

curtains
le tendine

venetian
blinds
le persiane

poster
il cartellone

chimney
il camino

roof
il tetto

armchair
la poltrona

sofa
il divano

television
il televisore

radio
la radio

fireplace
il focolare

carpet
il tappeto

footstool
il posapiedi

telephone
il telefono

lamp
la lampada

dresser
la toletta

record
il disco

record player
il giradischi

compact disc
**il compact
disc**

videocassette player
il videoregistratore

bedroom
**la camera
da letto**

bathroom
**la stanza
da bagno**

living room
il salotto

dining room
la sala da pranzo

kitchen
la cucina

cassette tape
la cassetta

cassette player
il magnetofono

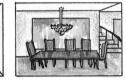

3. The Kitchen
La Cucina

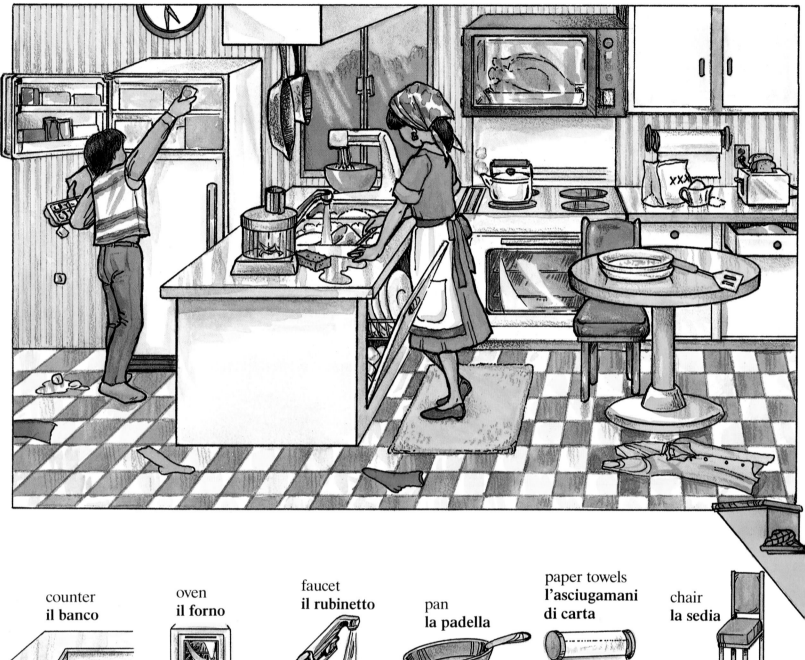

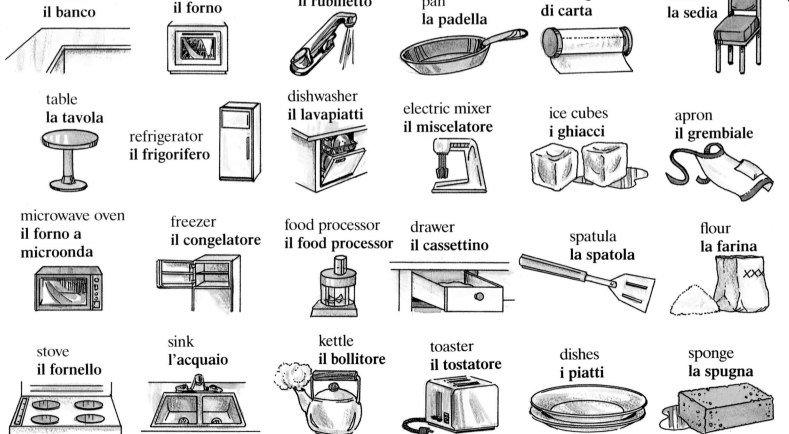

counter
il banco

oven
il forno

faucet
il rubinetto

pan
la padella

paper towels
**l'asciugamani
di carta**

chair
la sedia

table
la tavola

refrigerator
il frigorifero

dishwasher
il lavapiatti

electric mixer
il miscelatore

ice cubes
i ghiacci

apron
il grembiale

microwave oven
**il forno a
microonda**

freezer
il congelatore

food processor
il food processor

drawer
il cassettino

spatula
la spatola

flour
la farina

stove
il fornello

sink
l'acquaio

kettle
il bollitore

toaster
il tostatore

dishes
i piatti

sponge
la spugna

washing machine
la lavatrice

iron
il ferro da stiro

screw
la vite

toolbox
**la scatola
degli utensili**

laundry detergent
il detersivo

laundry
il bucato

broom
la scopa

mop
**la scopa
di stracci**

screwdriver
il cacciavite

wrench
la chiave

wood
il legno

board
la tavola

dustpan
**la paletta della
spazzatura**

electrical outlet
la presa

vacuum cleaner
l'aspirapolvere

drill
il trapano

sandpaper
la carta vetrata

flashlight
**la lampadina
tascabile**

hammer
il martello

brick
il mattone

ironing board
la tavola da stiro

nail
il chiodo

file
la lima

tape measure
il metro a nastro

saw
il saracco

clothes dryer
l'asciugatrice

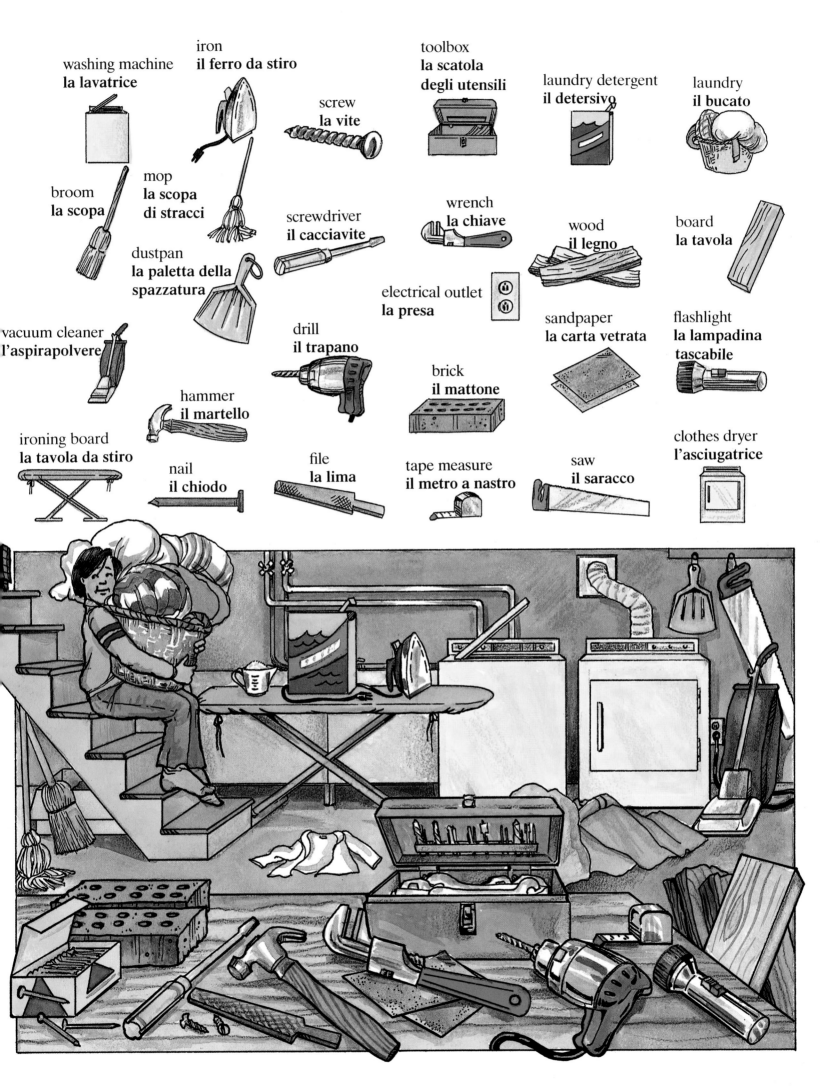

4. The Attic
La Soffitta

trunk
il baule

game
il gioco

coloring book
**il libro
di disegni**

box
la scatola

doll
la bambola

music box
**la scatola
della musica**

dust
il polvere

jigsaw puzzle
il rompicapo

yarn
la filaccia

string
lo spago

jump rope
la corda

knitting
needles
i ferri da calza

cobweb
la ragnatela

teddy bear
l'orsacchiotto

dollhouse
**la casa
da bambole**

ball gown
il veste da ballo

toys
i giocattoli

comic books
**i giornali
a fumetti**

top hat
**il cappello
a cilindro**

whistle
lo zufolo

lightbulb
la lampadina

tuxedo
l'abito nero

cards
le carte

toy soldiers
i piccoli soldati

hat
il cappello

movie projector
il proiettore

feather
la piuma

dice
i dadi

cowboy hat
**il cappello
di cowboy**

blocks
i blocchi

umbrella
l'ombrello

uniform
la divisa

electric train
il trenino

puppet
il burrattino

cowboy boots
**gli stivali
di cowboy**

magnet
il magnete

fan
il ventaglio

photo album
**l'album
di fotografie**

cradle
la culla

marbles
**le palline
di marmo**

rocking horse
il cavallo a dondolo

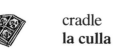

chess
**il gioco degli
scacchi**

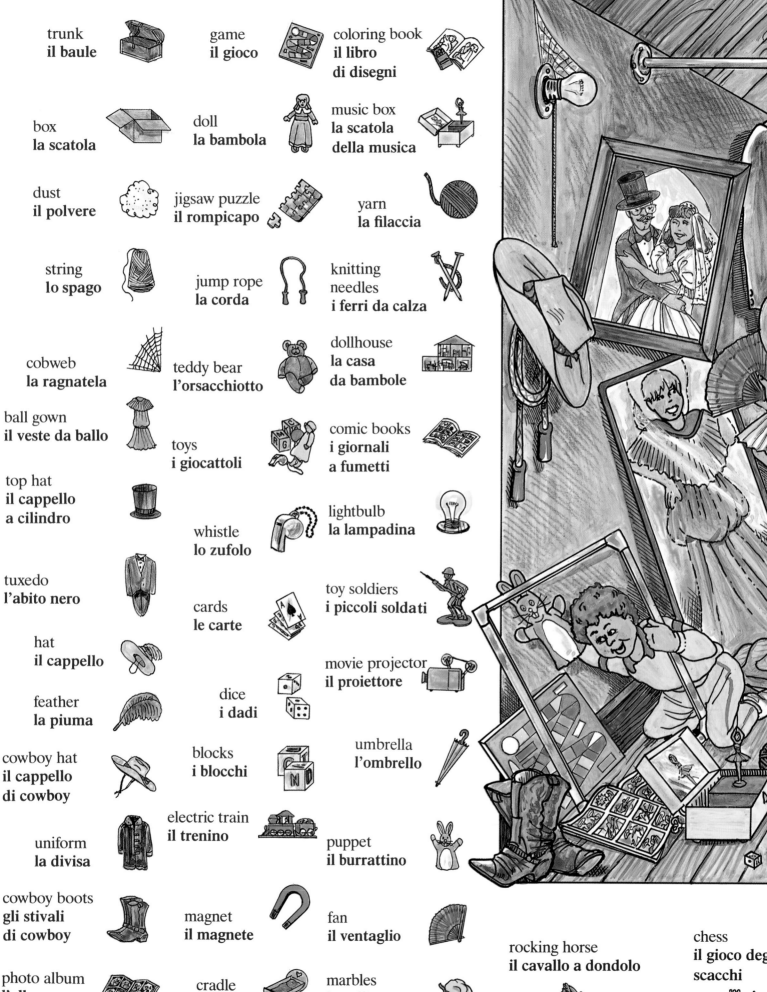

photograph
la foto

spinning wheel
il filatoio

picture frame
la cornice

rocking chair
la sedia a dondolo

checkers
il gioco della dama

5. The Four Seasons (Weather)
Le Quattro Stagioni (Il Tempo)

Winter
L'Inverno

snow
la neve

sled
la slitta

ice
il ghiaccio

snowplow
lo spazzaneve

snowflake
il fiocco di neve

snowmobile
il gatto delle nevi

icicle
il ghiacciolo

snowman
l'uomo di neve

shovel
la pala

snowball
la palotta di neve

snowstorm
il turbine di neve

log
il ceppo

Spring
La Primavera

rain
la pioggia

flowers
i fiori

rainbow
l'arcobaleno

flowerbed
l'aiuola

stem
lo stelo

petal
il petalo

bird
l'uccello

vegetable garden
l'orto

worm
il verme

raindrop
la goccia di pioggia

lightning
il fulmine

Summer
l'Estate

butterfly
la farfalla

lawn mower
la falciatrice meccanica

fly
la mosca

barbecue
la griglia

fly swatter
il chiappamosche

hammock
l'amaca

fan
il ventilatore

yard
il cortile

sprinkler
lo spruzzatore

deck
la veranda

grasshopper
la cavalletta

garden hose
l'idrante

matches
i fiammiferi

Fall
L'Autunno

wind
il vento

kite
l'aquilone

leaf
la foglia

puddle
la pozzanghera

branch
il ramo

mud
il fango

fog
la nebbia

bird's nest
il nido

rake
il rastrello

clouds
le nuvole

bush
il cespuglio

6. At the Supermarket   Al Supermercato

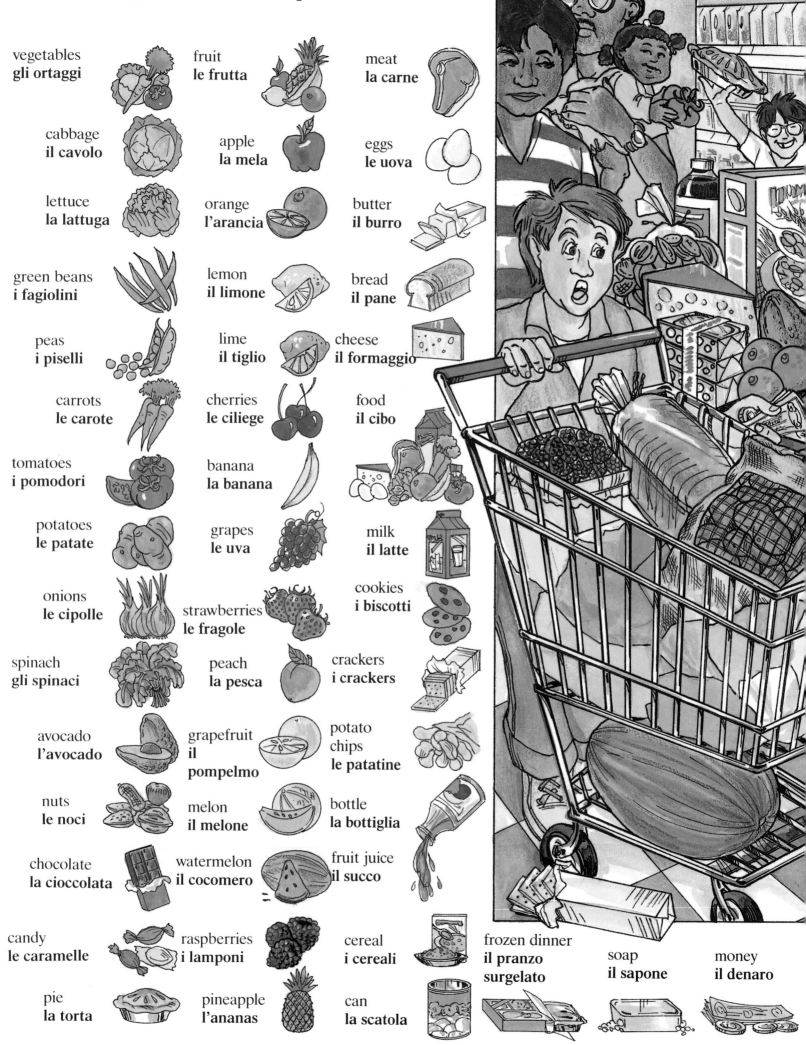

vegetables
gli ortaggi

cabbage
il cavolo

lettuce
la lattuga

green beans
i fagiolini

peas
i piselli

carrots
le carote

tomatoes
i pomodori

potatoes
le patate

onions
le cipolle

spinach
gli spinaci

avocado
l'avocado

nuts
le noci

chocolate
la cioccolata

candy
le caramelle

pie
la torta

fruit
le frutta

apple
la mela

orange
l'arancia

lemon
il limone

lime
il tiglio

cherries
le ciliege

banana
la banana

grapes
le uva

strawberries
le fragole

peach
la pesca

grapefruit
il pompelmo

melon
il melone

watermelon
il cocomero

raspberries
i lamponi

pineapple
l'ananas

meat
la carne

eggs
le uova

butter
il burro

bread
il pane

cheese
il formaggio

food
il cibo

milk
il latte

cookies
i biscotti

crackers
i crackers

potato chips
le patatine

bottle
la bottiglia

fruit juice
il succo

cereal
i cereali

can
la scatola

frozen dinner
il pranzo surgelato

soap
il sapone

money
il denaro

shopping cart
il carrello

shopping
bag
**il pacco
per la spesa**

sign
il cartellino

scale
la bilancia

price
il prezzo

cash register
la cassa

cashier
la cassiere

7. Clothing   Abiti

glasses
gli occhiali

buckle
la fibbia

belt
la cintura

collar
il collo

blouse
la camicetta

bracelet
il braccialetto

ring
l'anello

skirt
la gonna

pants
i pantaloni

socks
i calzini

shoes
le scarpe

underwear
**la biancheria
intima**

tie
la cravatta

necklace
la collana

sleeve
la manica

dress
il vestito

suit
il completo

bathing suit
il costume da bagno

shirt
la camicia

button
il bottone

earmuffs
il paraorecchie

gloves
i guanti

handkerchief
il fazzoletto

sweater
il golf

shoelace
la stringa

coat
il cappotto

gym shoes
le scarpe da tennis

tights
la calzamaglia

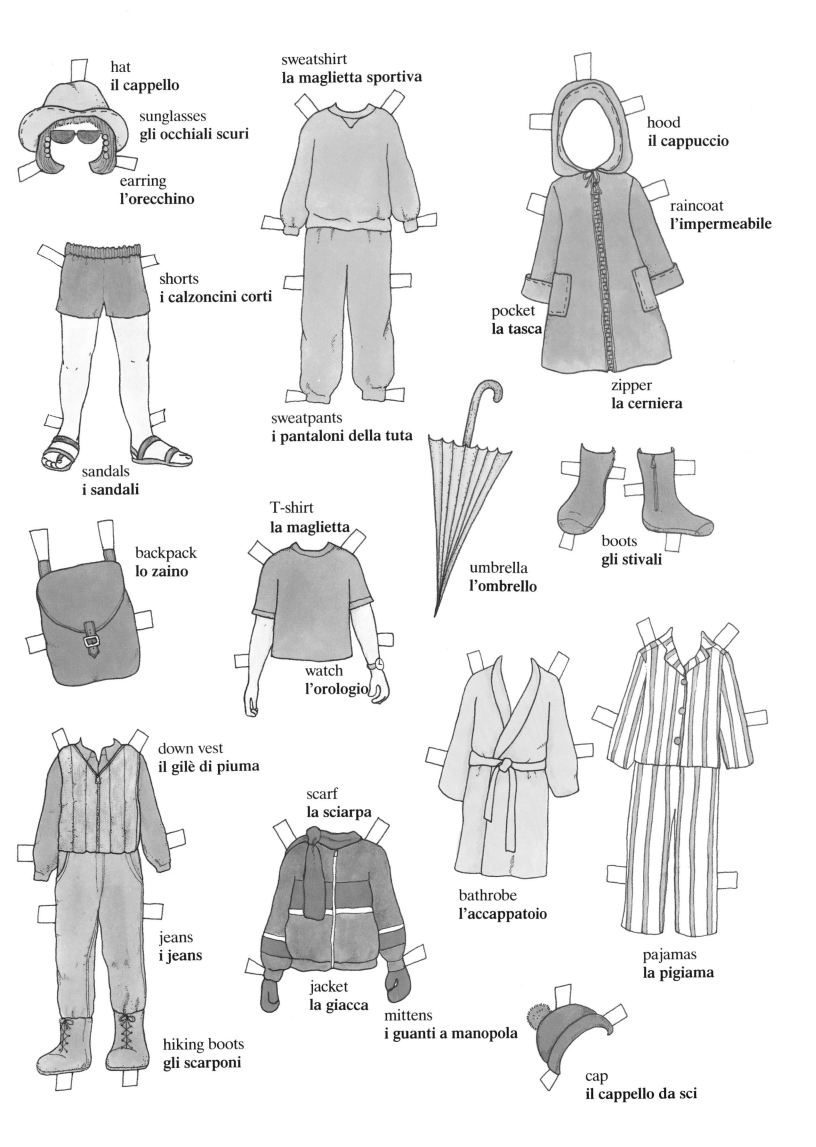

hat
il cappello

sunglasses
gli occhiali scuri

earring
l'orecchino

sweatshirt
la maglietta sportiva

hood
il cappuccio

raincoat
l'impermeabile

shorts
i calzoncini corti

pocket
la tasca

zipper
la cerniera

sandals
i sandali

sweatpants
i pantaloni della tuta

backpack
lo zaino

T-shirt
la maglietta

umbrella
l'ombrello

boots
gli stivali

watch
l'orologio

down vest
il gilè di piuma

scarf
la sciarpa

bathrobe
l'accappatoio

jeans
i jeans

pajamas
la pigiama

jacket
la giacca

mittens
i guanti a manopola

hiking boots
gli scarponi

cap
il cappello da sci

8. In the City   Nella Città

building
l'edificio

apartment building
l'edificio degli appartamenti

train station
la stazione

skyscraper
il grattacielo

fire escape
la scala di sicurezza

church
la chiesa

factory
la fabbrica

balcony
il balcone

school
la scuola

smokestack
il fumaiolo

fire station
la stazione dei pompieri

museum
il museo

traffic lights
il semaforo

police station
il posto di polizia

hospital
l'ospedale

manhole cover
la bocca di accesso

jail
il carcere

drugstore (pharmacy)
la farmacia

driveway
la strada privata

bookstore
la libreria

movie theater
il cinema

toy store
il negozio dei gioccattoli

parking lot
il parcheggio

restaurant
il ristorante

parking meter
il parchimetro

grocery store
la drogheria

clothing store
il negozio di confezioni

corner
l'angolo

bakery
la panetteria

fire hydrant
l'idrante

butcher shop
la macelleria

hotel
l'albergo

square
la piazza

fountain
la fontana

traffic jam
l'intasamento

statue
la statua

newspaper
il giornale

crane
la gru

bench
la panca

sign
il segnale

playground
il parco giochi

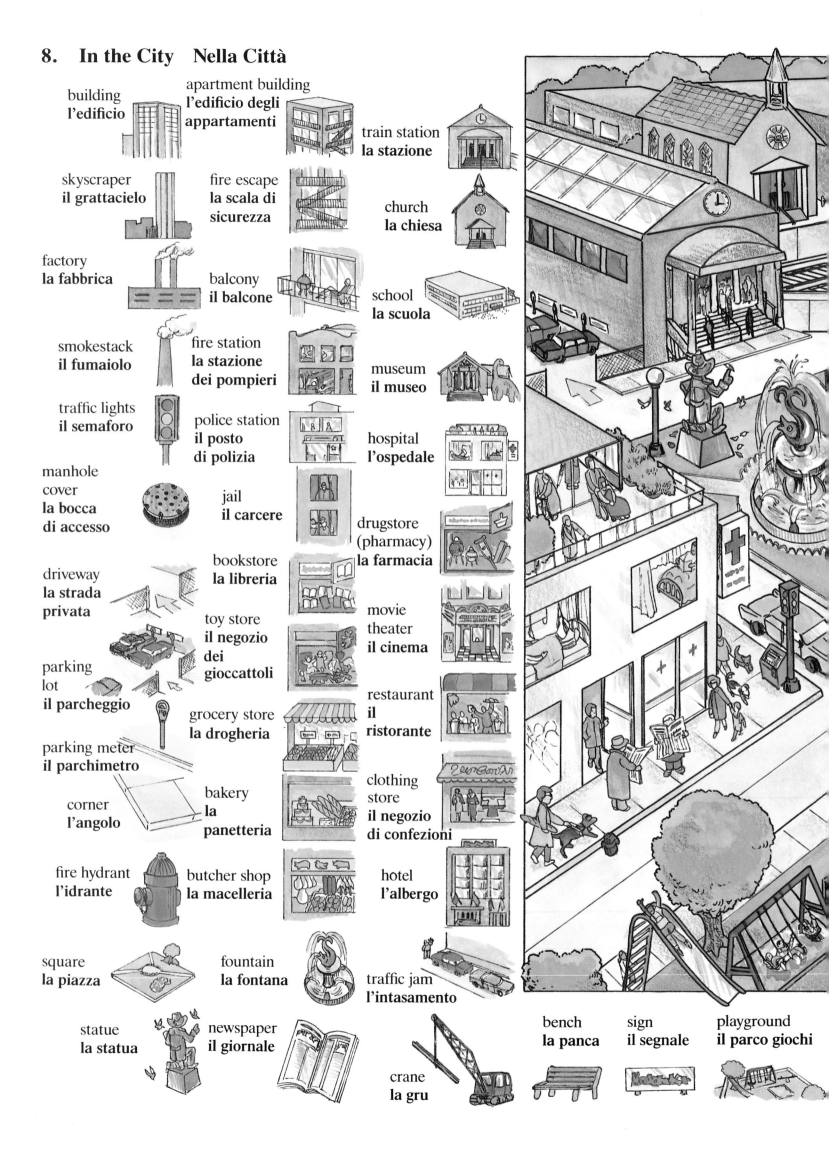

park	jungle gym	swings	seesaw	slide	sandbox	beach
il parco	**l'attrezzo ginnico**	**l'altalena**	**il su in giù**	**la scivola**	**il recinto con sabbia**	**la spiaggia**

9. In the Country In Paese

farmer
l'agricoltore

tractor
il trattore

barn
il granaio

hay
il fieno

dog
il cane

puppy
il cucciolo

cat
il gatto

kitten
il gattino

rooster
il gallo

hen
la gallina

chick
il pulcino

pig
il maiale

piglet
il porcellino

rabbit
il coniglio

bull
il toro

cow
la mucca

calf
il vitello

horse
il cavallo

colt
il puledro

duck
l'anitra

duckling
l'anatroccolo

goat
la capra

kid
il capretto

goose
l'oca

gosling
il papero

sheep
la pecora

lamb
l'agnello

mouse
il topo

horns
le corna

donkey
l'asino

bees
le api

frog
la rana

pond
lo stagno

grass
l'erba

fence
il recinto

tree
l'albero

shadow
l'ombra

hill
la collina

road
la strada

smoke
il fumo

picnic
il picnic

ant
la formica

dirt
la terra

tent
la tenda

sky
il cielo

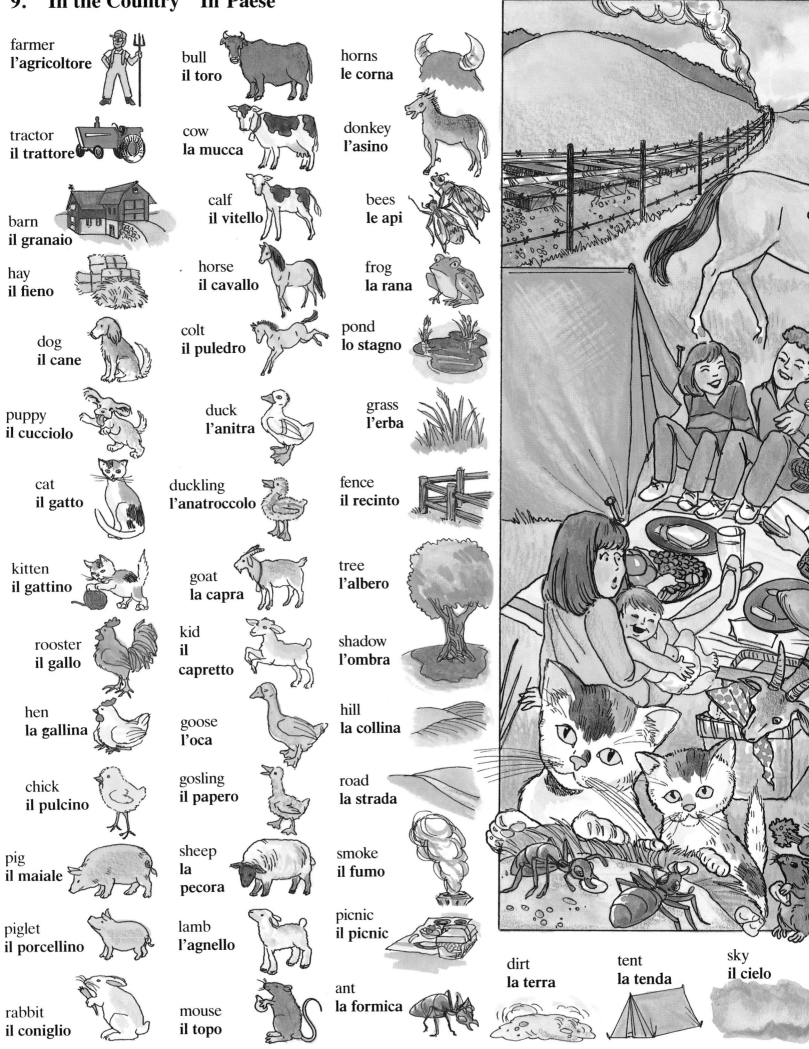

train tracks
le rotaie

sleeping bag
il sacco a pelo

man
l'uomo

woman
la donna

boy
il ragazzo

girl
la ragazza

baby
il piccino

farm
la fattoria

10. In a Restaurant Al Ristorante

breakfast **la colazione**

lunch **il pranzo**

dinner **la cena**

yolk **il rosso d'uovo**

hamburger **la svizzera**

steak **la bistecca**

omelet **la frittata**

sandwich **il tramezzino**

fish **il pesce**

toast **il crostino**

french fries **le patatine fritte**

ham **il prosciutto**

jam **la marmellata**

soup **la zuppa**

chicken **il pollo**

sausages **le salsiccie**

noodles **la pasta**

broccoli **i broccoletti**

coffee **il caffè**

ketchup **il ketchup**

celery **il sedano**

tea **il tè**

mustard **la mostarda**

salad **l'insalata**

cream **la panna**

salt **il sale**

rice **il riso**

sugar **lo zucchero**

pepper **il pepe**

mushroom **il fungo**

meals **i pasti**

ice cream **il gelato**

tray **il vassoio**

waiter **il cameriere**

candle **la candela**

tablecloth **la tovaglia**

waitress **la cameriera**

cake **la torta**

straw **la cannuccia**

gift **il regalo**

birthday party **la festa di compleanno**

soft drink **la bevanda**

knife **il coltello**

fork **la forchetta**

spoon **il cucchiaio**

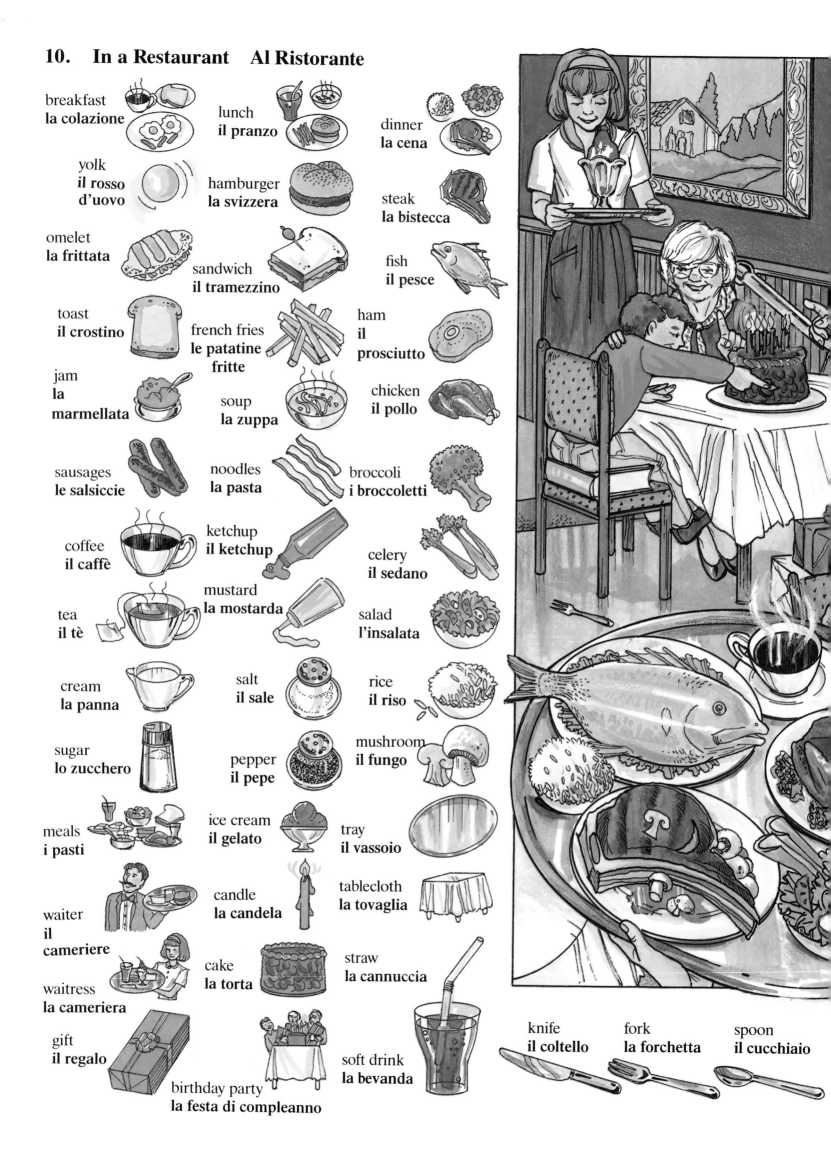

plate	saucer	cup	glass	bowl	napkin
il piatto	**il piattino**	**la tazza**	**il bicchiere**	**la scodella**	**il tovagliolo**

menu
il menù

11. The Doctor's Office   Dal Medico

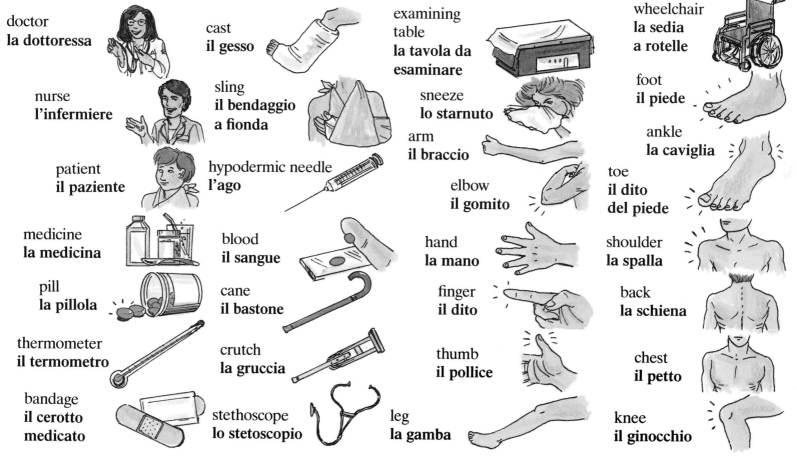

doctor
la dottoressa

nurse
l'infermiere

patient
il paziente

medicine
la medicina

pill
la pillola

thermometer
il termometro

bandage
**il cerotto
medicato**

cast
il gesso

sling
**il bendaggio
a fionda**

hypodermic needle
l'ago

blood
il sangue

cane
il bastone

crutch
la gruccia

stethoscope
lo stetoscopio

examining
table
**la tavola da
esaminare**

sneeze
lo starnuto

arm
il braccio

elbow
il gomito

hand
la mano

finger
il dito

thumb
il pollice

leg
la gamba

wheelchair
**la sedia
a rotelle**

foot
il piede

ankle
la caviglia

toe
**il dito
del piede**

shoulder
la spalla

back
la schiena

chest
il petto

knee
il ginocchio

The Dentist's Office   Dal Dentista

dentist
il dentista

waiting room
l'anticamera

eyebrow
il sopracciglio

braces
l'apparecchio per denti

dental hygienist
l'assistente del dentista

magazines
le riviste

eyes
gli occhi

head
la testa

tooth
il dente

X ray
i raggi X

nose
il naso

face
la faccia

toothbrush
lo spazzolino da denti

smile
il sorriso

mouth
la bocca

cheek
la guancia

toothpaste
il dentifricio

lips
le labbra

chin
il mento

forehead
la fronte

dental floss
la bavella

tongue
la lingua

ear
l'orecchio

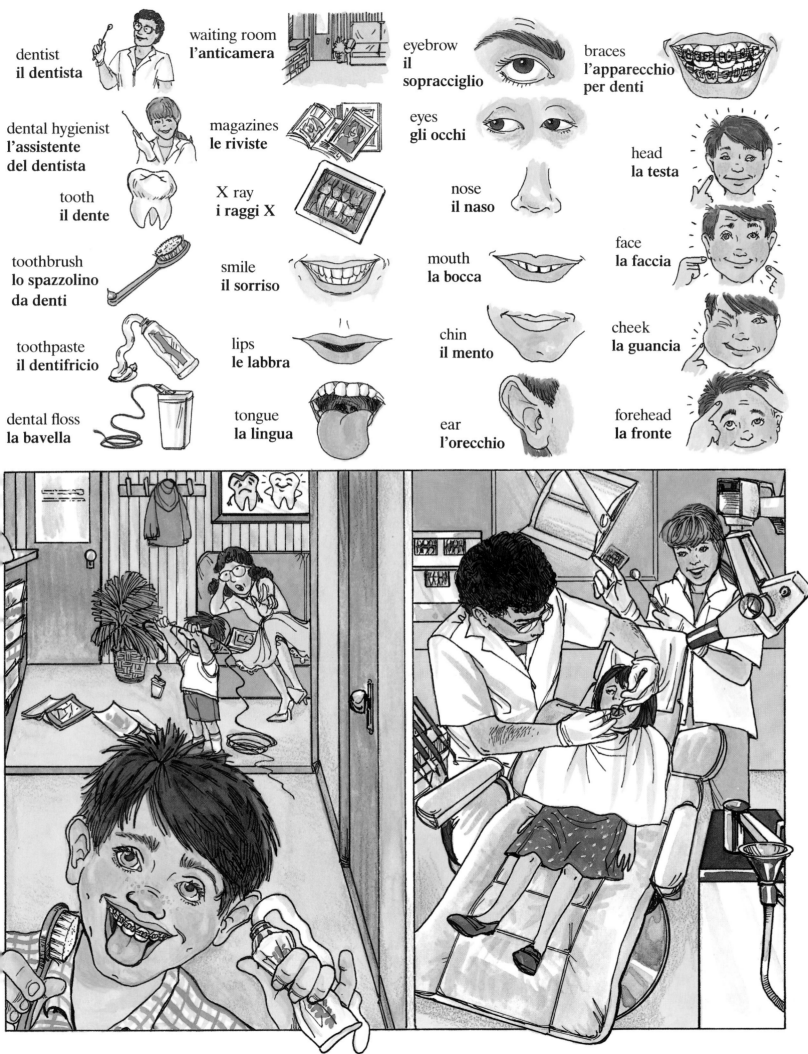

12. The Barber Shop/Beauty Salon
Dal Barbiere/Istituto di Bellezza

hairstylist
la parrucchiera

shampoo
lo shampoo

suds
la schiuma di sapone

comb
il pettine

brush
la spazzola

scissors
le forbici

curlers
i bigodini

curling iron
il ferro per arricciare i capelli

barber
il barbiere

shaving cream
la crema da barba

razor
il rasoio

beard
la barba

mousse
il mousse

manicurist
la manicure

fingernail
l'unghia

nail polish
lo smalto

lipstick
il rossetto

mascara
la mascara

powder
la cipra

hair dryer
l'asciugacapelli

bald
calvo

mustache
i baffi

freckles
le lentiggini

pedicurist
la pedicure

barrette
il fermacapelli

braid
la treccia

wavy
ondulati

straight
lisci

curly
ricci

short
corti

long
lunghi

black
neri

brown
castagni

blond
biondi

red
rossi

toenail
l'unghia del piede

nail clippers
il tagliaunghie

nail file
la limaiola

crew cut
il taglio a spazzola

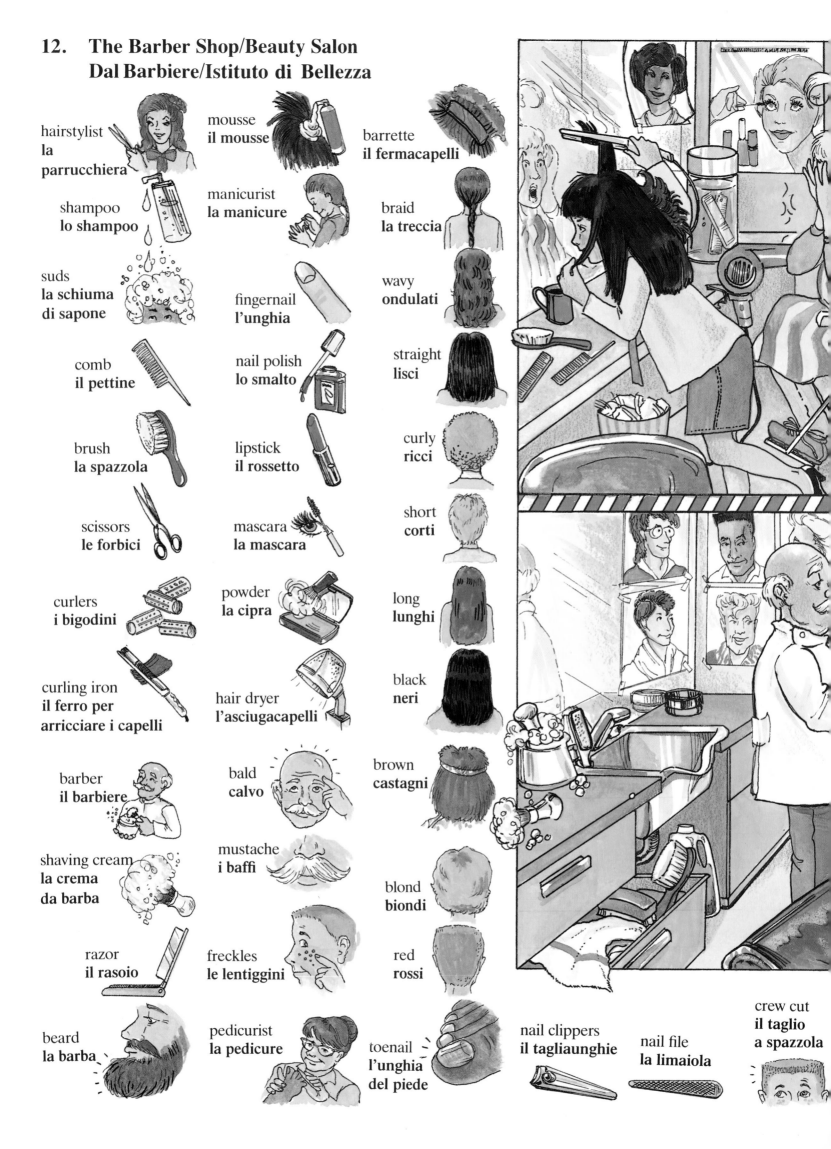

ponytail
la coda di cavallo

bangs
la frangia

bun
il chignon

part
la scriminatura

hair spray
lo spruzzo

hair
i capelli

blow dryer
il fon

13. The Post Office   L'Ufficio Postale

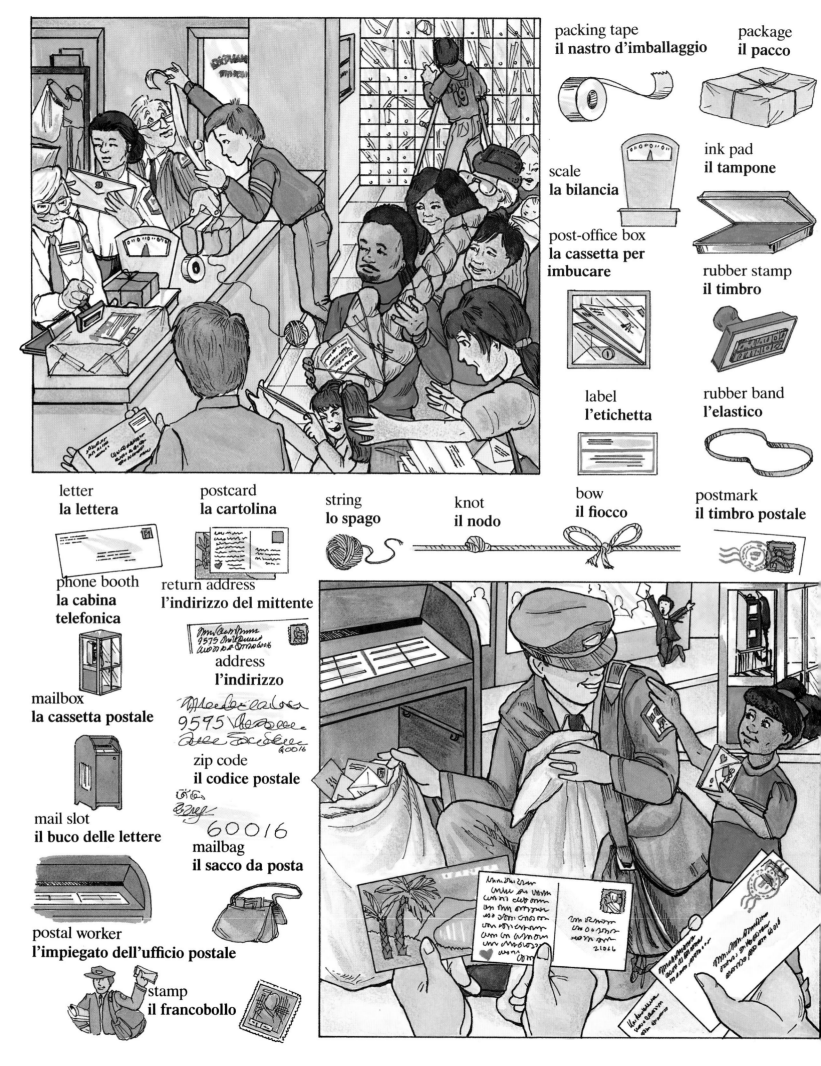

packing tape
il nastro d'imballaggio

package
il pacco

scale
la bilancia

ink pad
il tampone

post-office box
la cassetta per imbucare

rubber stamp
il timbro

label
l'etichetta

rubber band
l'elastico

letter
la lettera

postcard
la cartolina

string
lo spago

knot
il nodo

bow
il fiocco

postmark
il timbro postale

phone booth
la cabina telefonica

return address
l'indirizzo del mittente

address
l'indirizzo

mailbox
la cassetta postale

zip code
il codice postale

mail slot
il buco delle lettere

mailbag
il sacco da posta

postal worker
l'impiegato dell'ufficio postale

stamp
il francobollo

The Bank   La Banca

paper clip
la graffa

security guard
la guardia

security camera
**la telecamera
di sicurezza**

safe
la cassaforte

credit card
**la carta
di credito**

typewriter
**la macchina
da scrivere**

safety deposit box
**la cassetta
di sicurezza**

notepad
il blocco

wallet
il portafoglio

key
la chiave

lock
la serratura

file cabinet
lo schedario

teller
il cassiere

bill
il biglietto

coin
la mòneta

receptionist
la segretaria

check
l'assegno

checkbook
il libretto d'assegni

piggy bank
il salvadanaio

signature
la firma

drive-in
**il servizio per
le automobili**

automatic teller
il bancomat

14. At the Gas Station   Alla Stazione di Servizio

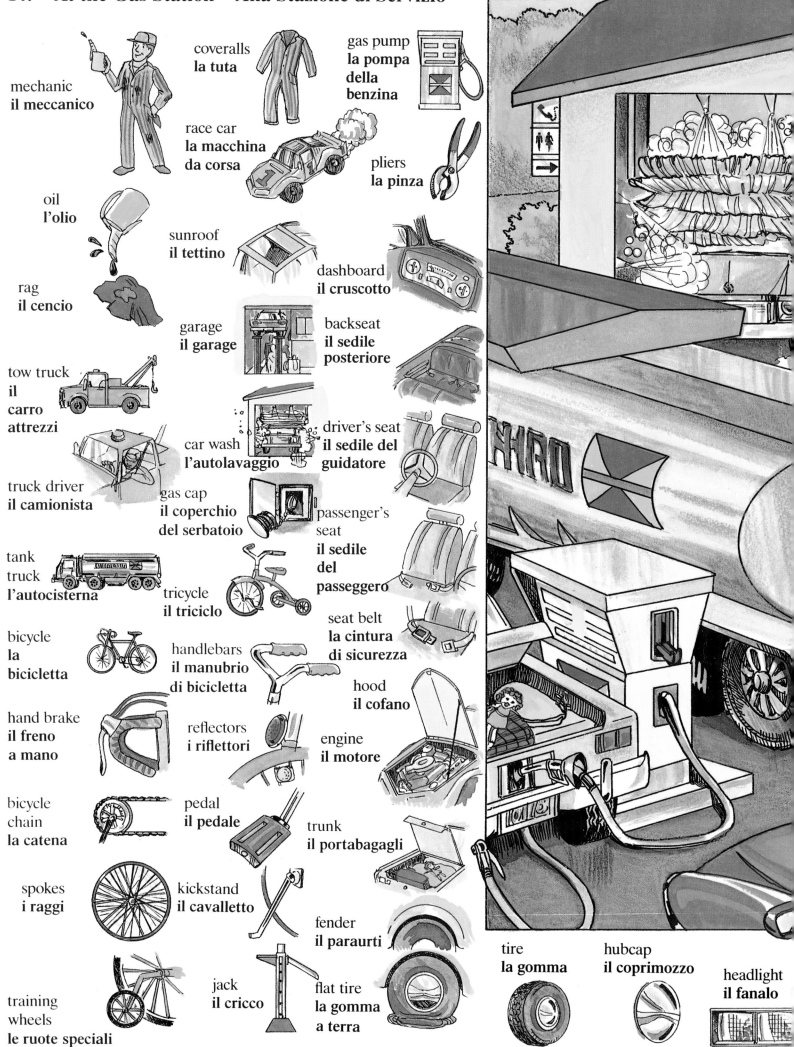

mechanic
il meccanico

coveralls
la tuta

gas pump
la pompa della benzina

race car
la macchina da corsa

pliers
la pinza

oil
l'olio

sunroof
il tettino

dashboard
il cruscotto

rag
il cencio

garage
il garage

backseat
il sedile posteriore

tow truck
il carro attrezzi

car wash
l'autolavaggio

driver's seat
il sedile del guidatore

truck driver
il camionista

gas cap
il coperchio del serbatoio

passenger's seat
il sedile del passeggero

tank truck
l'autocisterna

tricycle
il triciclo

seat belt
la cintura di sicurezza

bicycle
la bicicletta

handlebars
il manubrio di bicicletta

hood
il cofano

hand brake
il freno a mano

reflectors
i riflettori

engine
il motore

bicycle chain
la catena

pedal
il pedale

trunk
il portabagagli

spokes
i raggi

kickstand
il cavalletto

fender
il paraurti

training wheels
le ruote speciali

jack
il cricco

flat tire
la gomma a terra

tire
la gomma

hubcap
il coprimozzo

headlight
il fanalo

brake lights
le luci dei freni

windshield
il parabrezza

windshield wipers
il tergicristallo

steering wheel
il volante

rearview mirror
lo specchietto retrovisore

air hose
il manicotto dell'aria

door handle
la maniglia

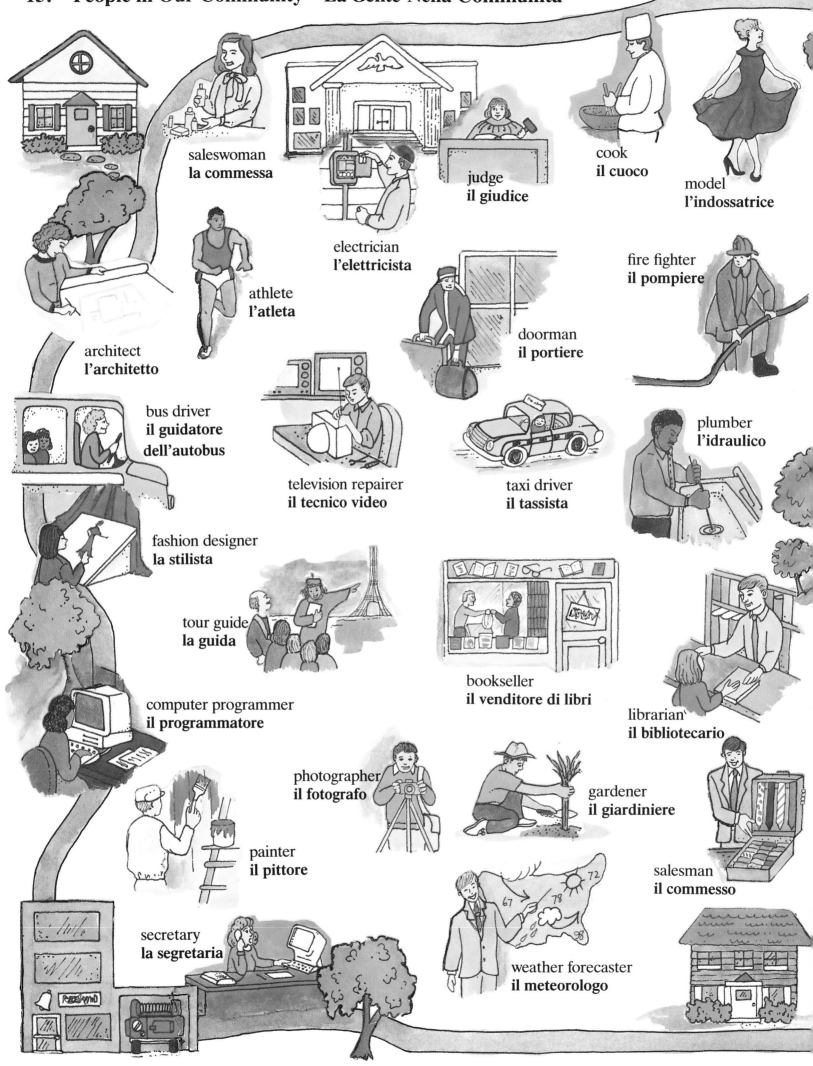

saleswoman
la commessa

judge
il giudice

cook
il cuoco

model
l'indossatrice

electrician
l'elettricista

athlete
l'atleta

architect
l'architetto

doorman
il portiere

fire fighter
il pompiere

bus driver
il guidatore dell'autobus

plumber
l'idraulico

television repairer
il tecnico video

taxi driver
il tassista

fashion designer
la stilista

tour guide
la guida

bookseller
il venditore di libri

computer programmer
il programmatore

librarian
il bibliotecario

photographer
il fotografo

gardener
il giardiniere

painter
il pittore

salesman
il commesso

secretary
la segretaria

weather forecaster
il meteorologo

veterinarian
il veterinario

policewoman
la donna poliziotto

disc jockey
il disc jockey

reporter
il cronista

construction worker
il manovale

florist
la fiorista

tailor
il sarto

factory worker
l'operaia

optician
l'ottico

butcher
il macellaio

jeweler
il gioielliere

foreman
il capomastro

carpenter
il falegname

banker
il banchiere

artist
l'artista

pharmacist
la farmacista

sailor
il marinaio

lawyer
l'avvocatessa

paramedic
l'assistente del medico

letter carrier
il postino

fisherman
il pescatore

cowboy
il cowboy

policeman
il poliziotto

astronomer
l'astronomo

16. Going Places (Transportation) Trasporto

car
la macchina

airplane
l'aereo

jeep
il jeep

hot-air balloon
il pallone

van
il furgone

hang glider
l'aliante

scooter
il monopattino

sail
la vela

helicopter
l'elicottero

skateboard
lo skateboard

sailboat
la barca a vela

rowboat
la barca a remi

roller skates
**i pattini
a rotelle**

tugboat
il rimorchiatore

canoe
la canoa

cruise ship
la nave

train
il treno

motorboat
il motoscafo

blimp
il dirigibile

taxi
il tassì

police car
**la macchina
da polizia**

camper
il camper

stroller
il passeggino

truck
il camion

bicycle
la bicicletta

baby
carriage
la carrozzina

fire engine
l'autopompa

traffic lights
il semaforo

cement
mixer
la betoniera

ambulance
il prontosoccorso

Stop!
stop

motorcycle
**la
motocicletta**

Wait!
aspetta

bus
l'autobus

street
la strada

intersection
l'incrocio

sidewalk
il marciapiede

school bus
l'autobus per scuola

lighthouse
il faro

Go!
avanti

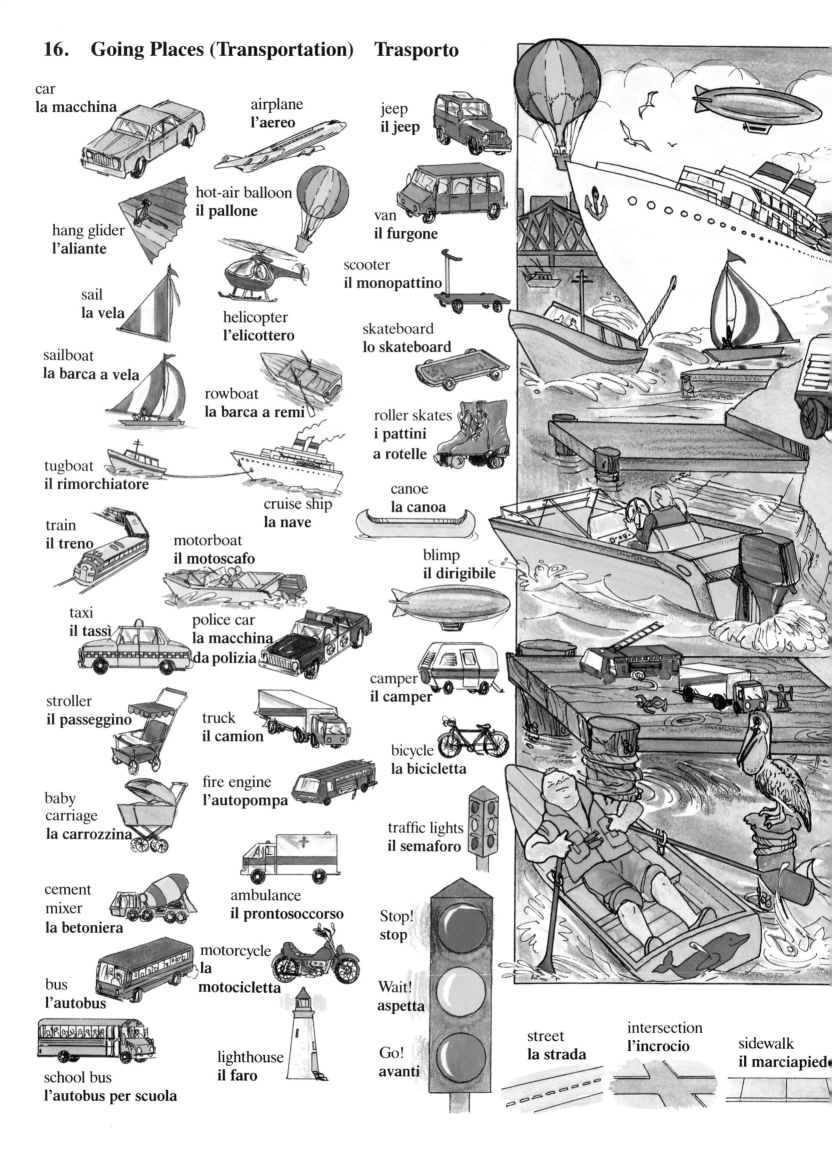

dock
il molo

bus stop
la fermata

bridge
il ponte

crosswalk
**il passaggio
pedonale**

oar
il remo

boat
la barca

stop sign
lo stop

17. The Airport   L'Aeroporto

pilot
il pilota

air-traffic controller
il controllore di volo

airplane
l'aereo

copilot
la seconda pilota

headset
la cuffia

propeller
l'elica

navigator
il navigatore

control tower
la torre di controllo

wing
l'ala

flight attendant
l'assistente di volo

radar screen
lo schermo di radar

engine
il motore

baggage handler
il portabaglio

flags
le bandiere

landing gear
il carrello d'atterraggio

porter
il facchino

elevator
l'ascensore

runway
la pista

baggage claim
il ritiro bagagli

metal detector
il revelatore del metallo

hangar
l'aviorimessa

baggage check-in
lo sportello bagagli

escalator
la scala mobile

Concorde
il Concorde

ticket counter
lo sportello dei biglietti

gate
la porta

luggage compartment
il deposito bagagli

baggage cart
il carrello per bagagli

seat
il sedile

ticket agent
il bigliettaio

customs officer
l'agente doganale

passenger
il passeggero

ticket
il biglietto

snack bar
la tavola calda

passport
il passaporto

video camera
il video camera

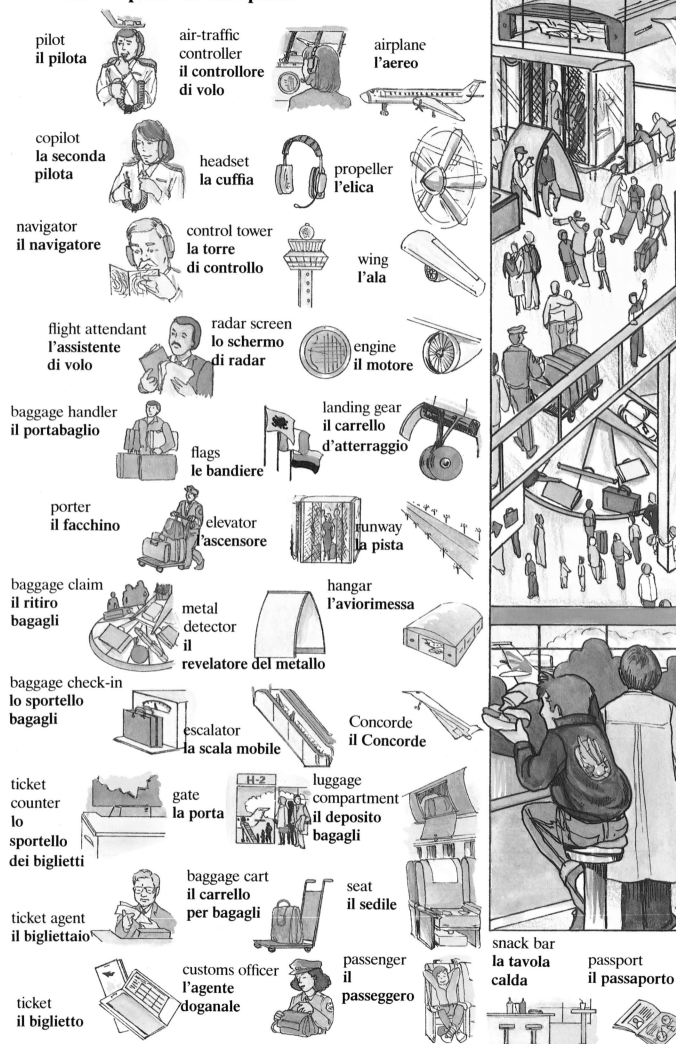

tennis racket
la racchetta

binoculars
il binocolo

camera
la macchina fotografica

purse
la borsa

suitcase
la valigia

garment bag
il sacco per abiti

briefcase
la borsa per documenti

18. Sports Sport

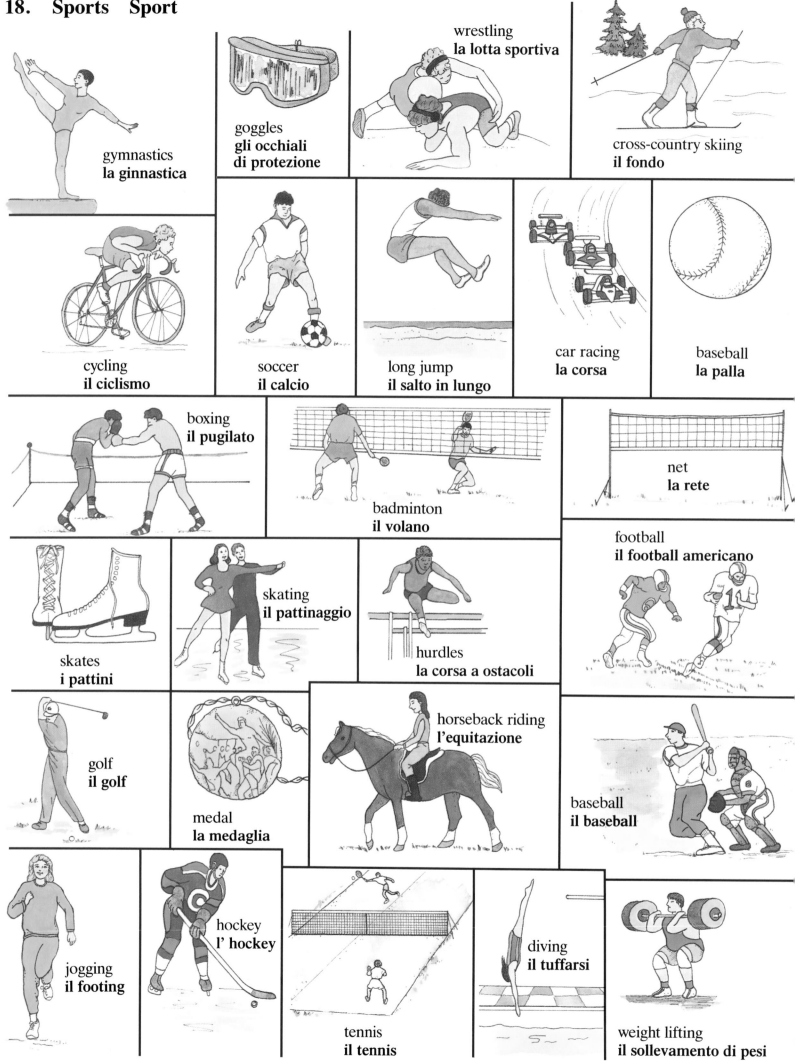

gymnastics
la ginnastica

goggles
**gli occhiali
di protezione**

wrestling
la lotta sportiva

cross-country skiing
il fondo

cycling
il ciclismo

soccer
il calcio

long jump
il salto in lungo

car racing
la corsa

baseball
la palla

boxing
il pugilato

badminton
il volano

net
la rete

football
il football americano

skates
i pattini

skating
il pattinaggio

hurdles
la corsa a ostacoli

golf
il golf

medal
la medaglia

horseback riding
l'equitazione

baseball
il baseball

jogging
il footing

hockey
l' hockey

tennis
il tennis

diving
il tuffarsi

weight lifting
il sollevamento di pesi

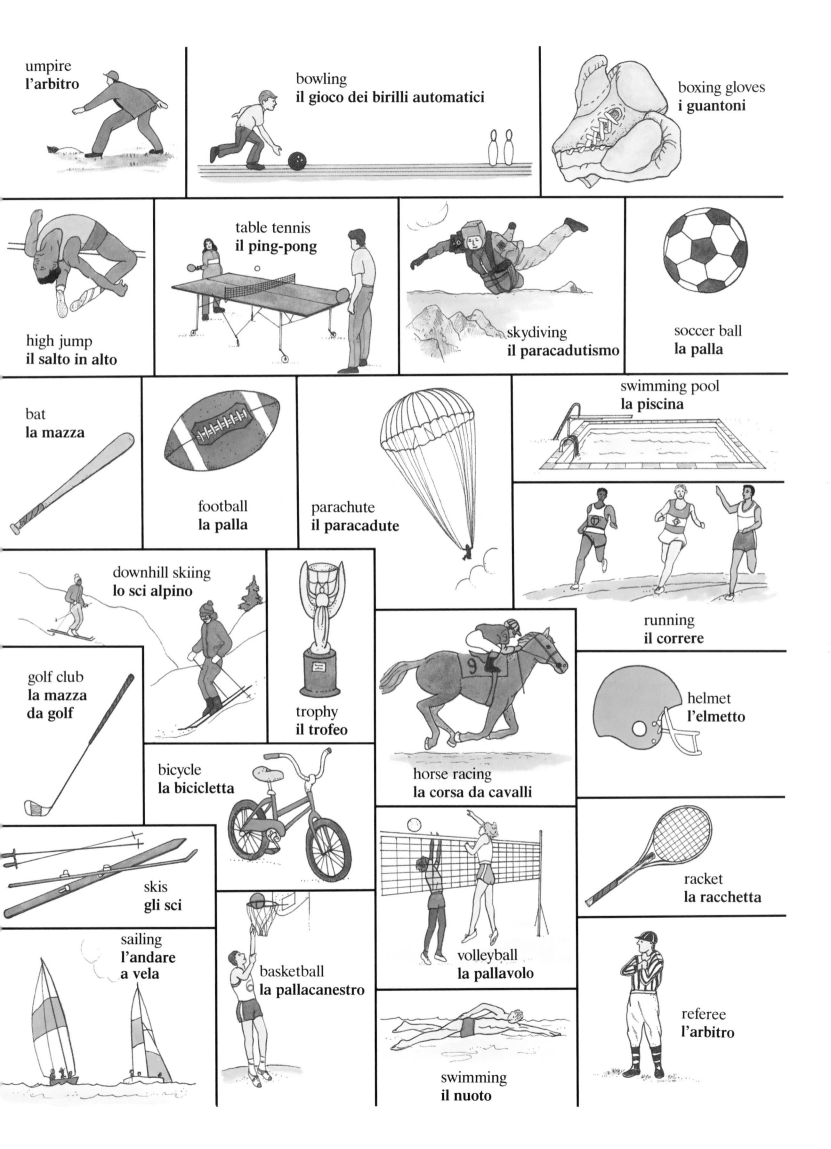

umpire
l'arbitro

bowling
il gioco dei birilli automatici

boxing gloves
i guantoni

high jump
il salto in alto

table tennis
il ping-pong

skydiving
il paracadutismo

soccer ball
la palla

bat
la mazza

football
la palla

parachute
il paracadute

swimming pool
la piscina

downhill skiing
lo sci alpino

trophy
il trofeo

running
il correre

golf club
**la mazza
da golf**

horse racing
la corsa da cavalli

helmet
l'elmetto

bicycle
la bicicletta

skis
gli sci

volleyball
la pallavolo

racket
la racchetta

sailing
**l'andare
a vela**

basketball
la pallacanestro

swimming
il nuoto

referee
l'arbitro

19. The Talent Show   La Mostra dei Talenti

actor **l'attore**

actress **l'attrice**

children **i ragazzi**

auditorium **l'auditorio**

audience **il pubblico**

singer **il cantante**

stage **il palcoscenico**

curtain **il sipario**

dancer **la ballerina**

scenery **il scenario**

script **il copione**

ballet slippers **le scarpette da ballo**

spotlight **il fascio di luce**

dressing room **il camerino**

tutu **il tutù**

rope **la corda**

sewing machine **la macchina per cucire**

leotard **la calzamaglia**

microphone **il microfono**

master of ceremonies **il cerimoniere**

costume **il costume**

makeup **il trucco**

orchestra pit **la buca dell' orchestra**

mask **la maschera**

sheet music **le carte di musica**

orchestra **l'orchestra**

wig **la parrucca**

conductor **il direttore d'orchestra**

accordion **la fisarmonica**

cymbals **i piatti**

trumpet **la tromba**

French horn **il cornetto**

saxophone **il sassofono**

xylophone **il silofono**

violin **il violino**

bow **l'archetto**

guitar **la chitarra**

drum **il tamburo**

piano **il pianoforte**

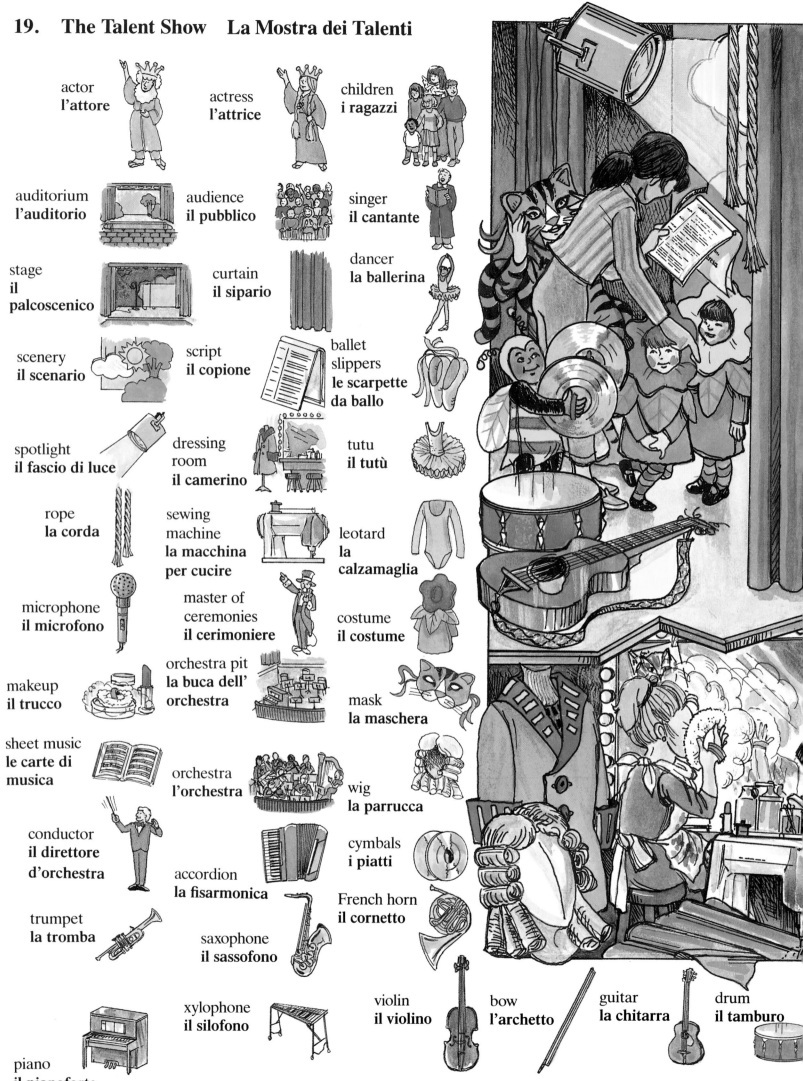

tuba
la tuba

flute
il flauto

trombone
il trombone

clarinet
il clarinetto

cello
il violoncello

strings
la corda

harp
l'arpa

20. At the Zoo   Allo Zoo

zookeeper
lo zoologo

elephant
l'elefante

animals
gli animali

rhinoceros
il rinoceronte

ostrich
lo struzzo

fox
la volpe

lion
il leone

bear
l'orso

wolf
il lupo

tiger
la tigre

bear cub
l'orsacchiotto

alligator
il coccodrillo

tiger cub
il tigrotto

polar bear
l'orso bianco

zebra
la zebra

jaguar
il giaguaro

panda
l'orso panda

giraffe
la giraffa

leopard
il gattopardo

gorilla
il gorilla

monkey
la scimmia

flamingo
il fenicottero

parrot
il pappagallo

hippopotamus
l'ippopotamo

owl
il gufo

snake
il serpente

kangaroo
il canguro

swan
il cigno

seal
la foca

deer
il cervo

penguin
il pinguino

walrus
il tricheco

lizard
la lucertola

peacock
il pavone

hump
la gobba

turtle
la tartaruga

eagle
l'aquila

camel
il cammello

horns
le corna

wings
le ali

feathers
le piume

beak
il becco

paw
la zampa

claws
l'artiglio

mane
la criniera

tail
la coda

hoof
lo zoccolo

stripes
le striscie

spots
le macchie

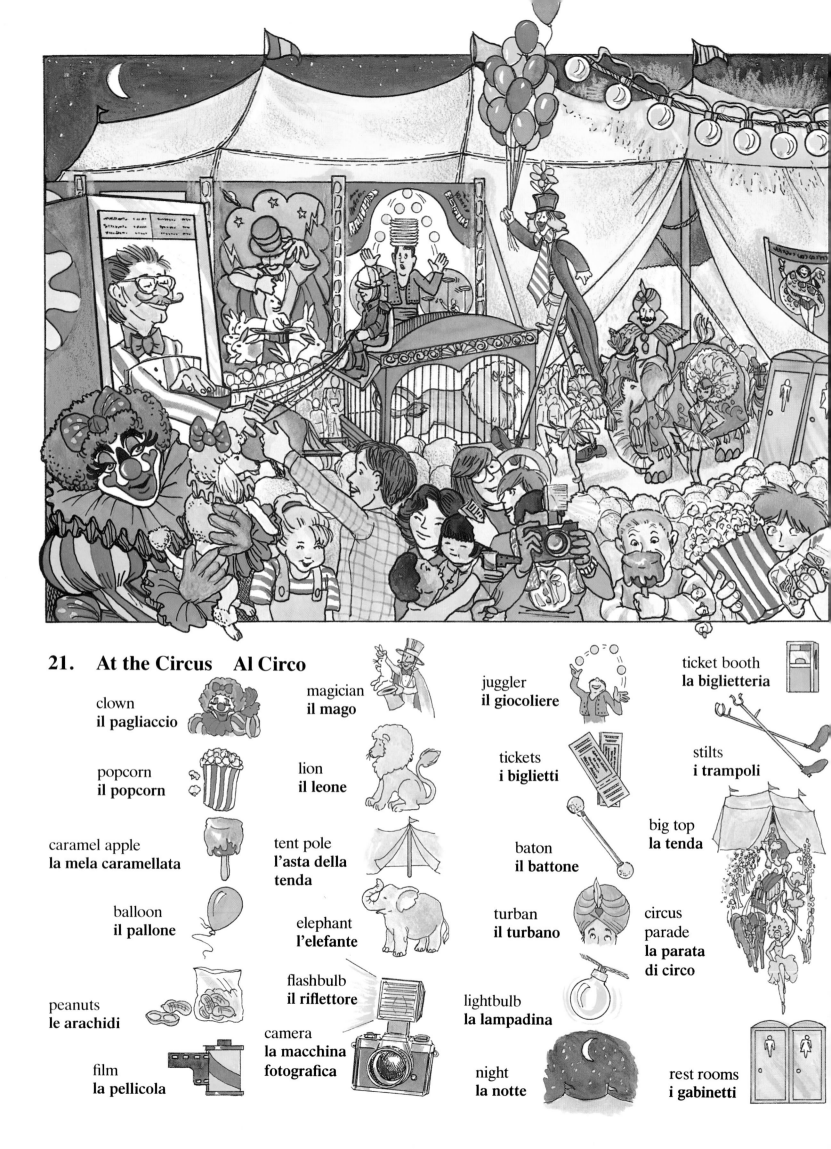

21. At the Circus   Al Circo

clown
il pagliaccio

magician
il mago

juggler
il giocoliere

ticket booth
la biglietteria

popcorn
il popcorn

lion
il leone

tickets
i biglietti

stilts
i trampoli

caramel apple
la mela caramellata

tent pole
l'asta della tenda

baton
il battone

big top
la tenda

balloon
il pallone

elephant
l'elefante

turban
il turbano

circus parade
la parata di circo

peanuts
le arachidi

flashbulb
il riflettore

lightbulb
la lampadina

camera
la macchina fotografica

film
la pellicola

night
la notte

rest rooms
i gabinetti

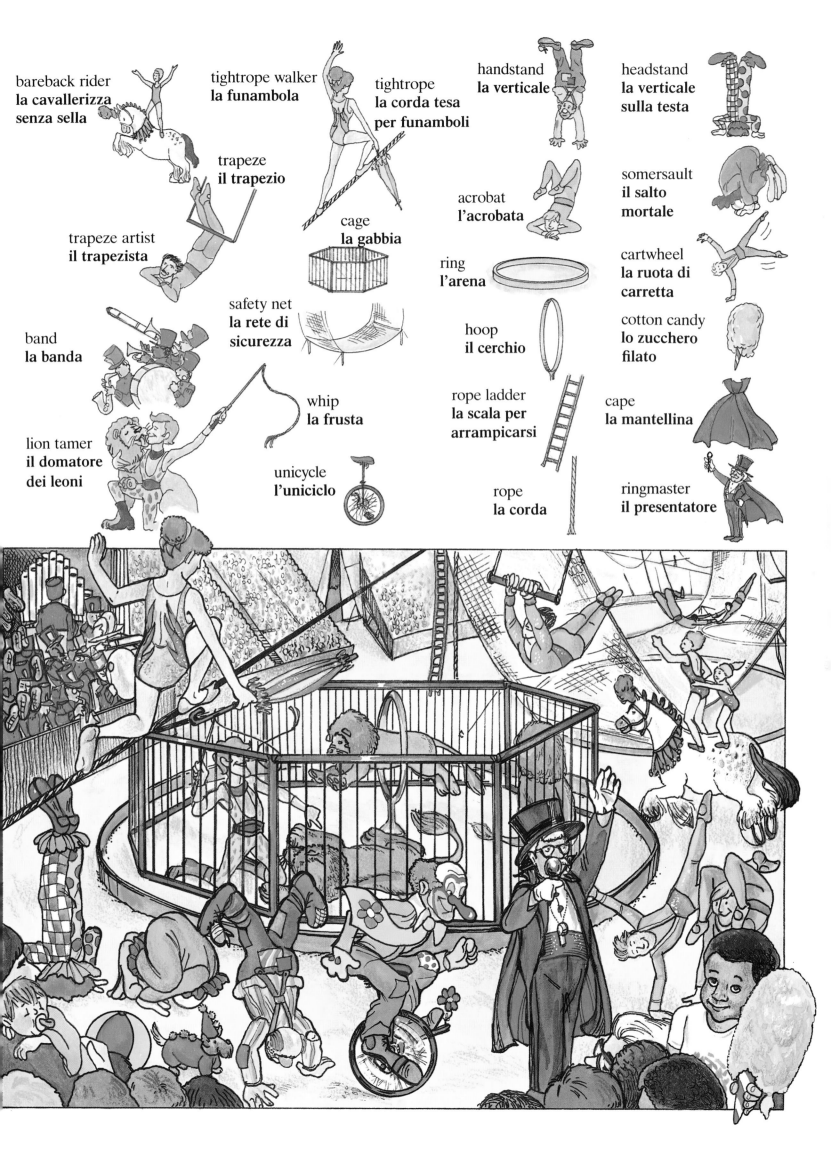

bareback rider
**la cavallerizza
senza sella**

tightrope walker
la funambola

tightrope
**la corda tesa
per funamboli**

handstand
la verticale

headstand
**la verticale
sulla testa**

trapeze
il trapezio

acrobat
l'acrobata

somersault
**il salto
mortale**

trapeze artist
il trapezista

cage
la gabbia

ring
l'arena

cartwheel
**la ruota di
carretta**

band
la banda

safety net
**la rete di
sicurezza**

hoop
il cerchio

cotton candy
**lo zucchero
filato**

whip
la frusta

rope ladder
**la scala per
arrampicarsi**

cape
la mantellina

lion tamer
**il domatore
dei leoni**

unicycle
l'uniciclo

rope
la corda

ringmaster
il presentatore

22. In the Ocean
L'Oceano

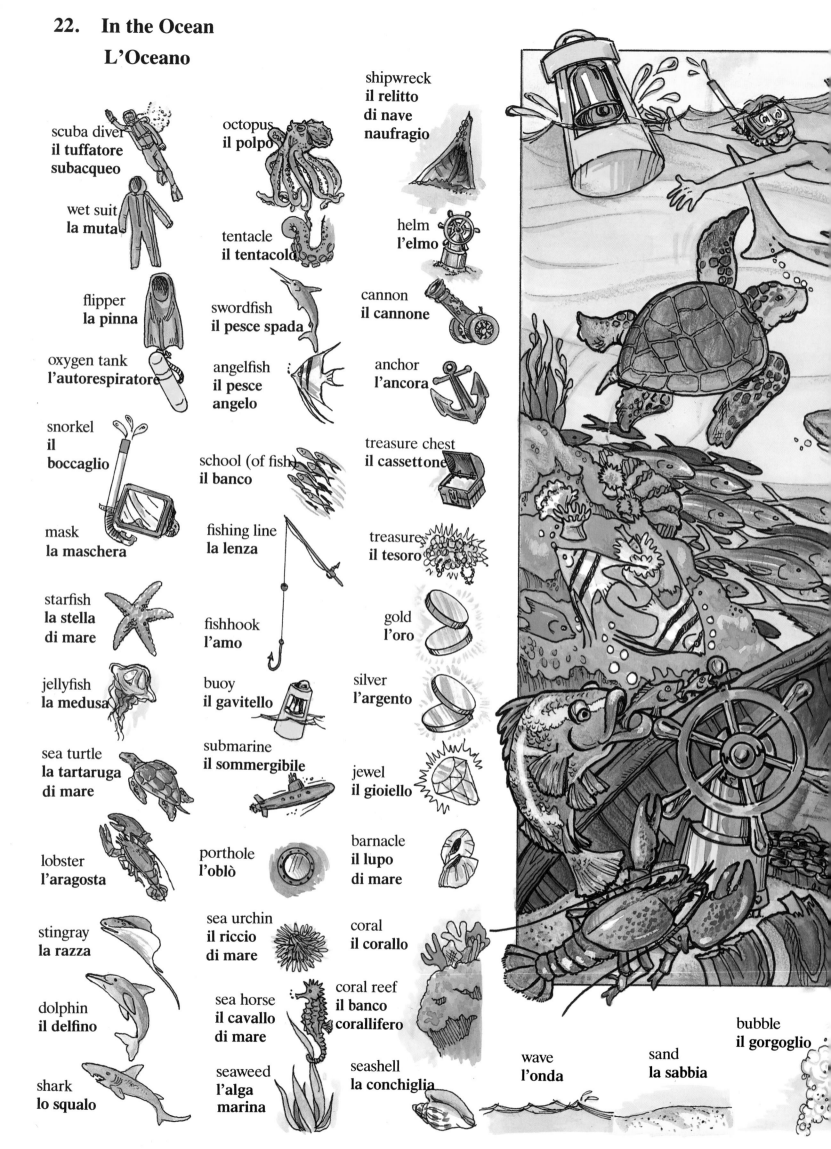

scuba diver
**il tuffatore
subacqueo**

wet suit
la muta

flipper
la pinna

oxygen tank
l'autorespiratore

snorkel
**il
boccaglio**

mask
la maschera

starfish
**la stella
di mare**

jellyfish
la medusa

sea turtle
**la tartaruga
di mare**

lobster
l'aragosta

stingray
la razza

dolphin
il delfino

shark
lo squalo

octopus
il polpo

tentacle
il tentacolo

swordfish
il pesce spada

angelfish
**il pesce
angelo**

school (of fish)
il banco

fishing line
la lenza

fishhook
l'amo

buoy
il gavitello

submarine
il sommergibile

porthole
l'oblò

sea urchin
**il riccio
di mare**

sea horse
**il cavallo
di mare**

seaweed
**l'alga
marina**

shipwreck
**il relitto
di nave
naufragio**

helm
l'elmo

cannon
il cannone

anchor
l'ancora

treasure chest
il cassettone

treasure
il tesoro

gold
l'oro

silver
l'argento

jewel
il gioiello

barnacle
**il lupo
di mare**

coral
il corallo

coral reef
**il banco
corallifero**

seashell
la conchiglia

wave
l'onda

sand
la sabbia

bubble
il gorgoglio

scales
le scaglie

gills
le branchie

fin
la pinna

clam
l'ostrica

crab
il granchio

squid
il calamaro

whale
la balena

23. Space
Lo Spazio

astronaut
l'astronauta

space suit
la tuta spaziale

space helmet
l'elmo spaziale

footprint
l'orma

space walk
il passeggio nello spazio

moon rock
il cristallo di luna

space shuttle
la navicella spaziale

lunar rover
la macchina lunare

laboratory
il laboratorio

cargo bay
la merce imbarcata

landing capsule
la capsula spaziale

scientist
lo scienziato

control panel
il pannello di controllo

ladder
la scala a pioli

lab coat
il camice

satellite
il satellite

space station
la stazione spaziale

microscope
il microscopio

spaceship
l'astronave

solar panel
il pannello solare

computer
il computer

alien
l'extraterreste

meteor shower
la pioggia dei meteori

beaker
l'alambicco

antenna
l'antenna

test tube
la provetta

constellation
la costellazione

asteroid
l'asteroide

solar system
il sistema solare

galaxy
la galassia

Earth
la Terra

the moon
la luna

the sun
il sole

planet
il pianeta

rings
i circoli

crater
il cratere

stars
le stelle

comet
la cometa

nebula
la nebulosa

rocket
il missile

robot
il robot

24. Human History

La Storia Umana

rock
la roccia

boulder
il masso
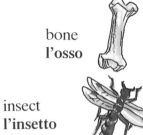

bone
l'osso

insect
l'insetto

fern
la felce

tree
l'albero

cave
la caverna

fur
la pelliccia

fire
il fuoco

stick
il bastoncino

wheel
la ruota

flint
la selce

arrowhead
**la punta
di freccia**

club
il bastone

spear
la lancia

mammoth
il mammùt

tusk
la zanna

trunk
la proboscide

bison
il bisonte

paint
il colore

cave drawing
**il disegno
di caverna**

hut
la capanna

corn
il granturco

wheat
il grano

weaver
la tessitrice

loom
il telaio

kiln
la fornace

potter
il vasaio

pot
il vaso

clay
l'argilla

cart
il carro

basket
la cesta

leather
il cuoio

fishing
la pesca

hunter
il cacciatore

well
il pozzo

bucket
la secchia

water
l'acqua

cloth
il panno

saber-toothed tiger
la tigre preistorica

crop
la raccolta

field
il camp

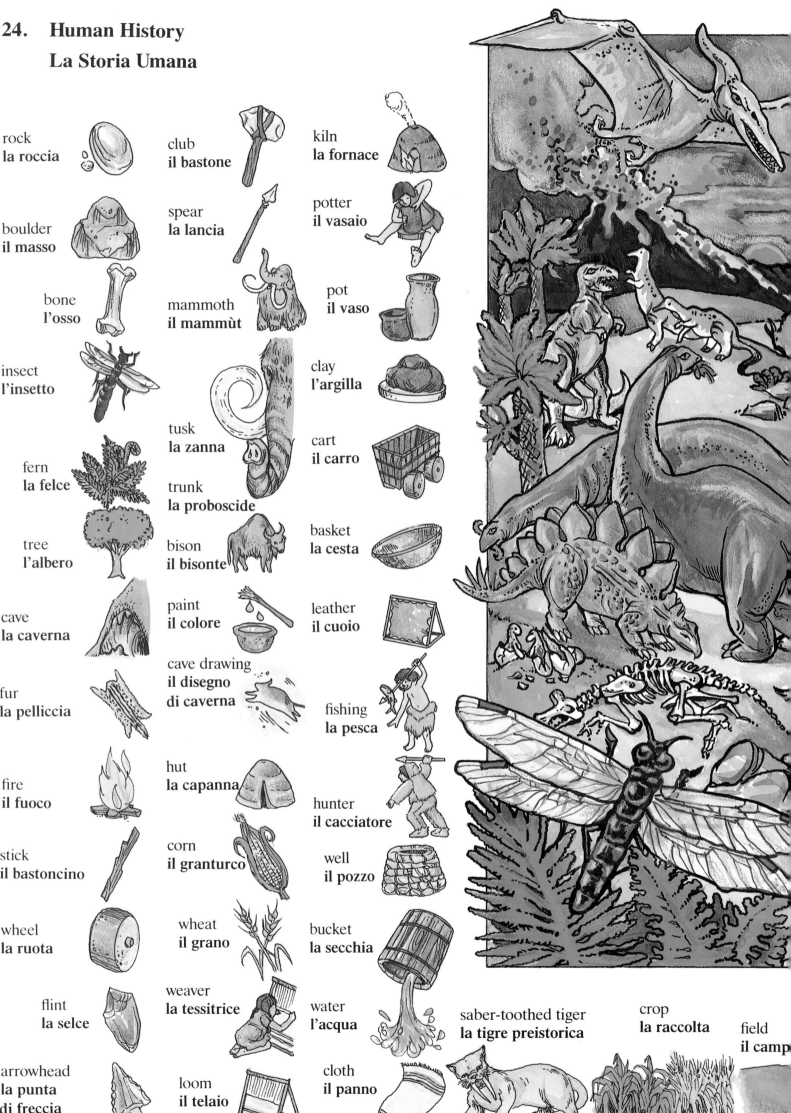

village
il villaggio

cave dwellers
i cavernicoli

skeleton
lo scheletro

dinosaur
il dinosauro

pterodactyl
il pterodattilo

25. The Make-Believe Castle Il Castello Immaginato

banner
lo stendardo

squire
lo scudiero

court jester
il burlone

dragon
il drago

knight
il cavaliere

minstrel
il menestrello

magic wand
**la bacchetta
magica**

armor
la corazza

unicorn
l'unicorno

fairy
la maga

chain mail
**la maglia
di ferro**

lance
la lancia

elf
l'elfo

shield
lo scudo

forest
la foresta

giant
il gigante

ax
l'accetta

saddle
la sella

forge
la fornace

stirrup
la staffa

sword
la spada

blacksmith
il fabbro ferraio

reins
le briglie

bow
l'arco

anvil
l'incudine

stable
la stalla

arrow
la freccia

horseshoe
**il ferro di
cavallo**

dungeon
**il carcere
sotterraneo**

quiver
la faretra

tower
la torre

moat
il fosso

archer
l'arciere

courtyard
il cortile

castle
il castello

drawbridge
**il ponte
levatoio**

bat
il pipistrello

rat
il ratto

crown
la corona

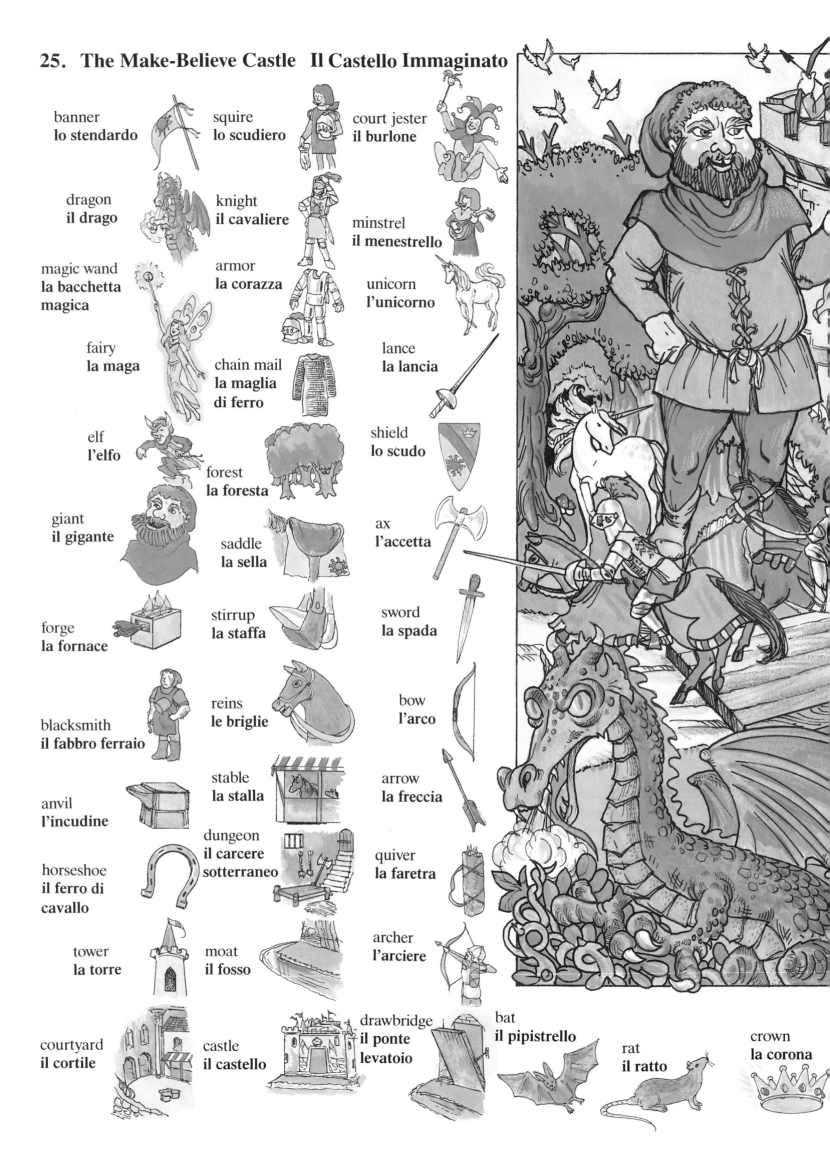

king
il re

queen
la regina

princess
la principessa

prince
il principe

throne
il trono

spider
il ragno

spiderweb
la ragnatela

26. The Mouse Hunt (Prepositions and Adjectives)
La Caccia al Topo (Preposizioni e Aggettivi)

behind
dietro

good
buono

above
sopra

on top of
su

in front of
davanti

inside
indietro

bad
male

outside
fuori

under
sotto

next to
vicino a

soft
morbido

tall
alto

wide
largo

narrow
stretto

short
basso

heavy
pesante

large
grande

difficult
difficile

medium
medio

dry
secco

small
piccolo

wet
umido

fat
grasso

full
pieno

empty
vuoto

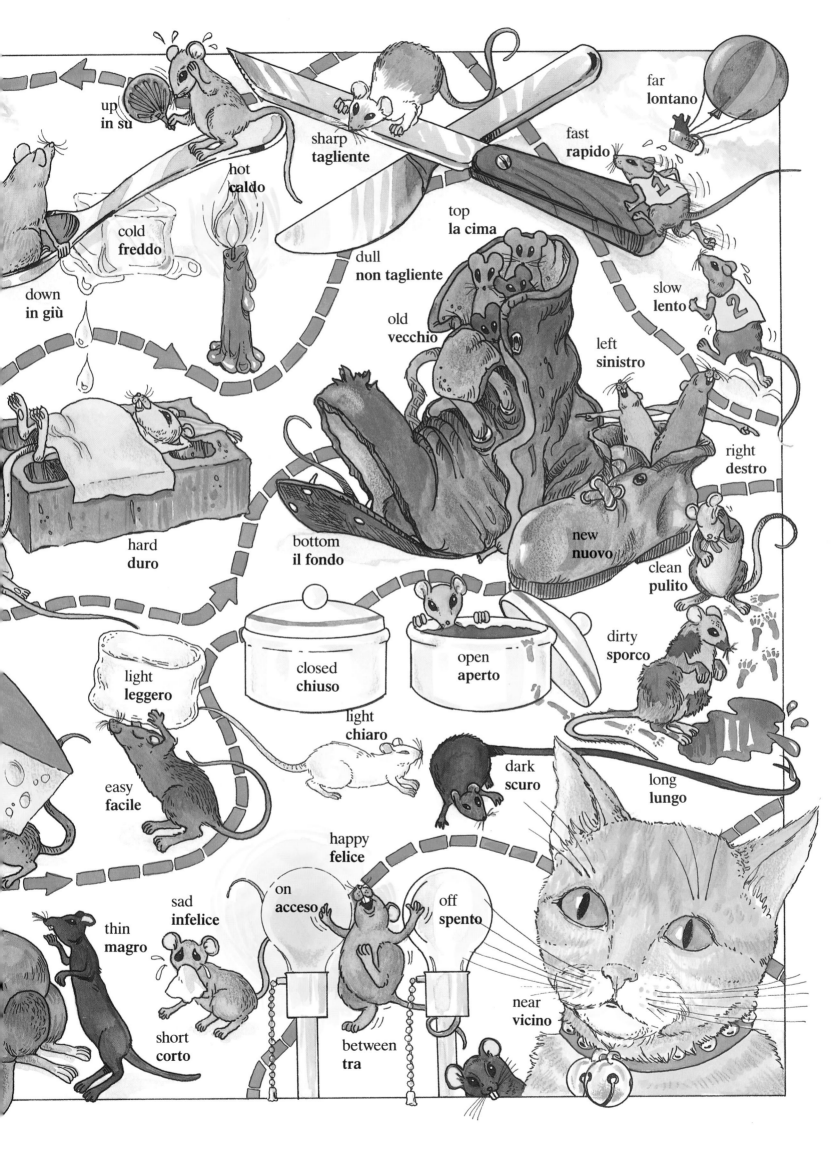

27. Action Words   Le Attività

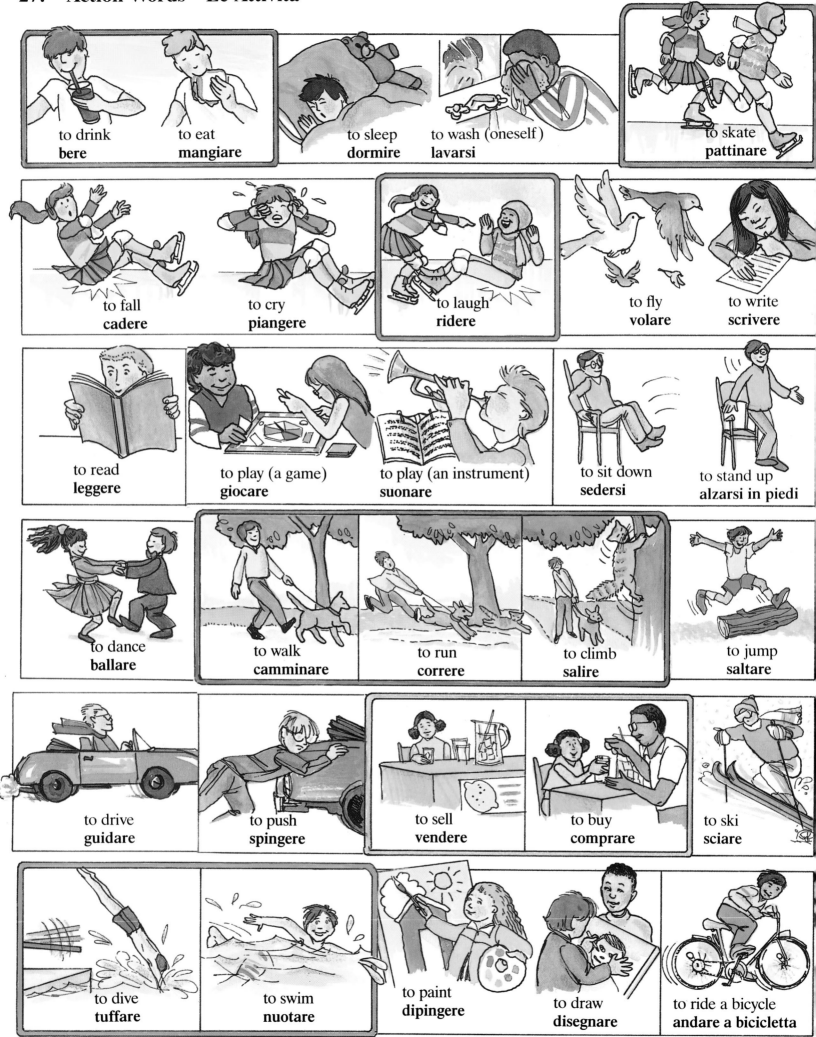

to drink **bere**

to eat **mangiare**

to sleep **dormire**

to wash (oneself) **lavarsi**

to skate **pattinare**

to fall **cadere**

to cry **piangere**

to laugh **ridere**

to fly **volare**

to write **scrivere**

to read **leggere**

to play (a game) **giocare**

to play (an instrument) **suonare**

to sit down **sedersi**

to stand up **alzarsi in piedi**

to dance **ballare**

to walk **camminare**

to run **correre**

to climb **salire**

to jump **saltare**

to drive **guidare**

to push **spingere**

to sell **vendere**

to buy **comprare**

to ski **sciare**

to dive **tuffare**

to swim **nuotare**

to paint **dipingere**

to draw **disegnare**

to ride a bicycle **andare a bicicletta**

to come
venire

to go
andare

to throw
gettare

to catch
prendere

to watch
guardare

to sing
cantare

to talk
parlare

to kick
dare un calcio

to listen (to)
ascoltare

to think
pensare

to roar
ruggire

to dig
scavare

to water
innaffiare

to juggle
fare giochi

to point (at)
mostrare

to look for
cercare

to find
trovare

to give
dare

to receive
ricevere

to cut
tagliare

to cook
cucinare

to open
aprire

to close
chiudere

to take a bath
bagnarsi

to teach
insegnare

to break
rompere

to fix
aggiustare

to carry
portare

to pull
tirare

to wait
aspettare

28. Colors Colori

white **bianco**

gray **grigio**

black **nero**

red **rosso**

purple **viola**

yellow **giallo**

green **verde**

pink **rosa**

orange **arancione**

brown **marrone**

blue **blu**

gold **dorato**

silver **argenteo**

29. The Family Tree L'Albero di Famiglia

grandmother, grandma **la nonna**

mother, mom **la madre** **la mamma**

father, dad **il padre** **il babbo**

son **il figlio**

brother **il fratello**

sister **la sorella**

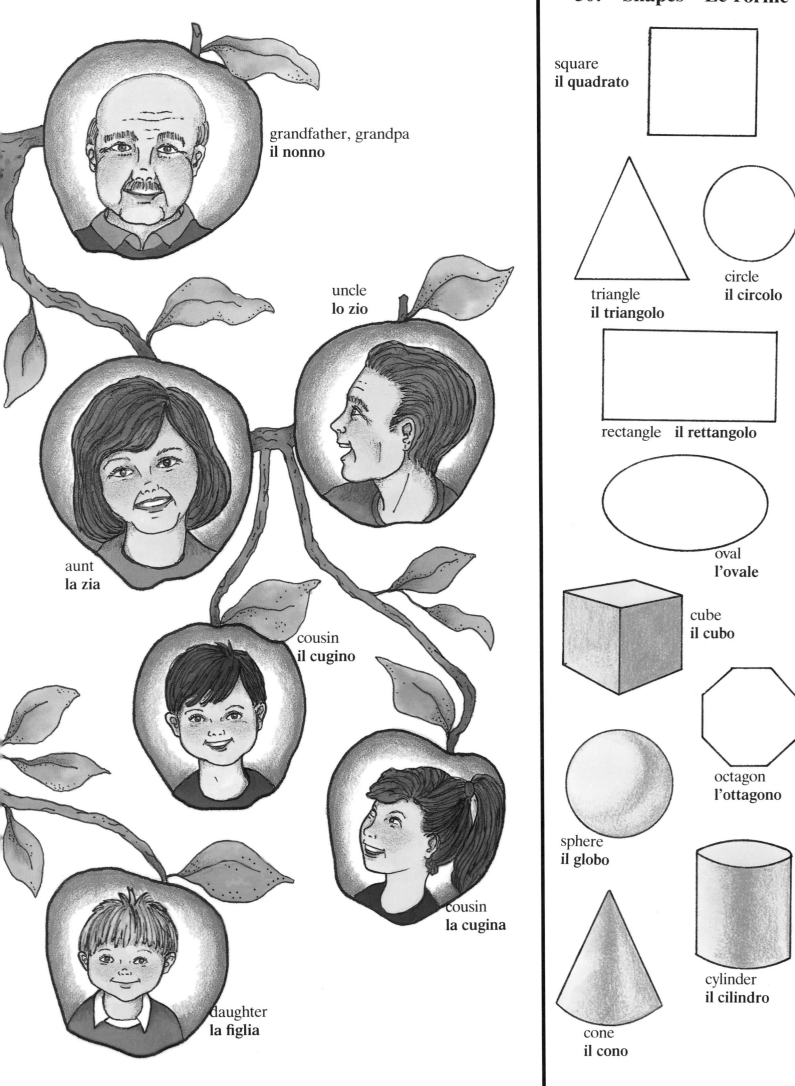

grandfather, grandpa
il nonno

uncle
lo zio

aunt
la zia

cousin
il cugino

cousin
la cugina

daughter
la figlia

square
il quadrato

triangle
il triangolo

circle
il circolo

rectangle   **il rettangolo**

oval
l'ovale

cube
il cubo

octagon
l'ottagono

sphere
il globo

cylinder
il cilindro

cone
il cono

31. Numbers I Numeri

Ordinal Numbers
I Numeri Ordinali

tenth
decimo

ninth
nono

eighth
ottavo

sixth
sesto

seventh
settimo

fourth
quarto

fifth
quinto

second
secondo

third
terzo

first
primo

Cardinal Numbers
I Numeri Cardinali

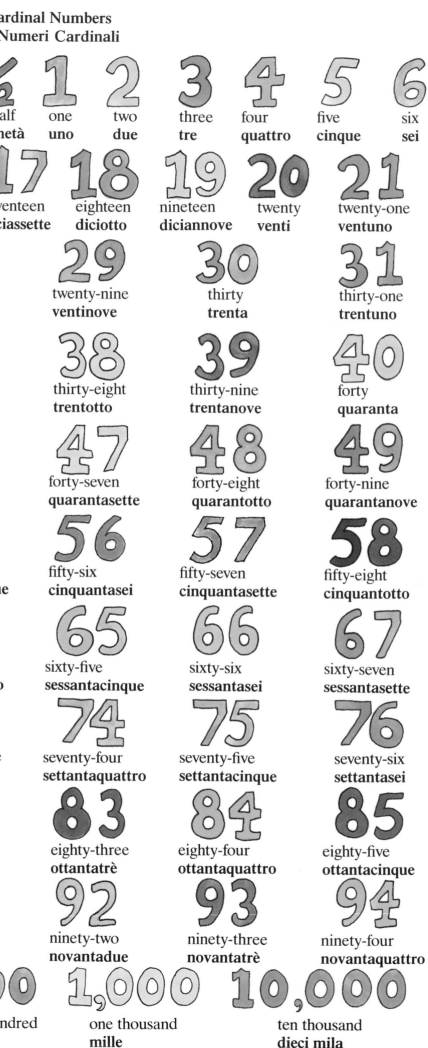

0 zero **lo zero**	½ one-half **una metà**	1 one **uno**	2 two **due**	3 three **tre**	4 four **quattro**	5 five **cinque**	6 six **sei**

16 sixteen **sedici**

17 seventeen **diciassette**

18 eighteen **diciotto**

19 nineteen **diciannove**

20 twenty **venti**

21 twenty-one **ventuno**

28 twenty-eight **ventotto**

29 twenty-nine **ventinove**

30 thirty **trenta**

31 thirty-one **trentuno**

37 thirty-seven **trentasette**

38 thirty-eight **trentotto**

39 thirty-nine **trentanove**

40 forty **quaranta**

46 forty-six **quarantasei**

47 forty-seven **quarantasette**

48 forty-eight **quarantotto**

49 forty-nine **quarantanove**

55 fifty-five **cinquantacinque**

56 fifty-six **cinquantasei**

57 fifty-seven **cinquantasette**

58 fifty-eight **cinquantotto**

64 sixty-four **sessantaquattro**

65 sixty-five **sessantacinque**

66 sixty-six **sessantasei**

67 sixty-seven **sessantasette**

73 seventy-three **settantatrè**

74 seventy-four **settantaquattro**

75 seventy-five **settantacinque**

76 seventy-six **settantasei**

82 eighty-two **ottantadue**

83 eighty-three **ottantatrè**

84 eighty-four **ottantaquattro**

85 eighty-five **ottantacinque**

91 ninety-one **novantuno**

92 ninety-two **novantadue**

93 ninety-three **novantatrè**

94 ninety-four **novantaquattro**

100 one hundred **cento**

1,000 one thousand **mille**

10,000 ten thousand **dieci mila**

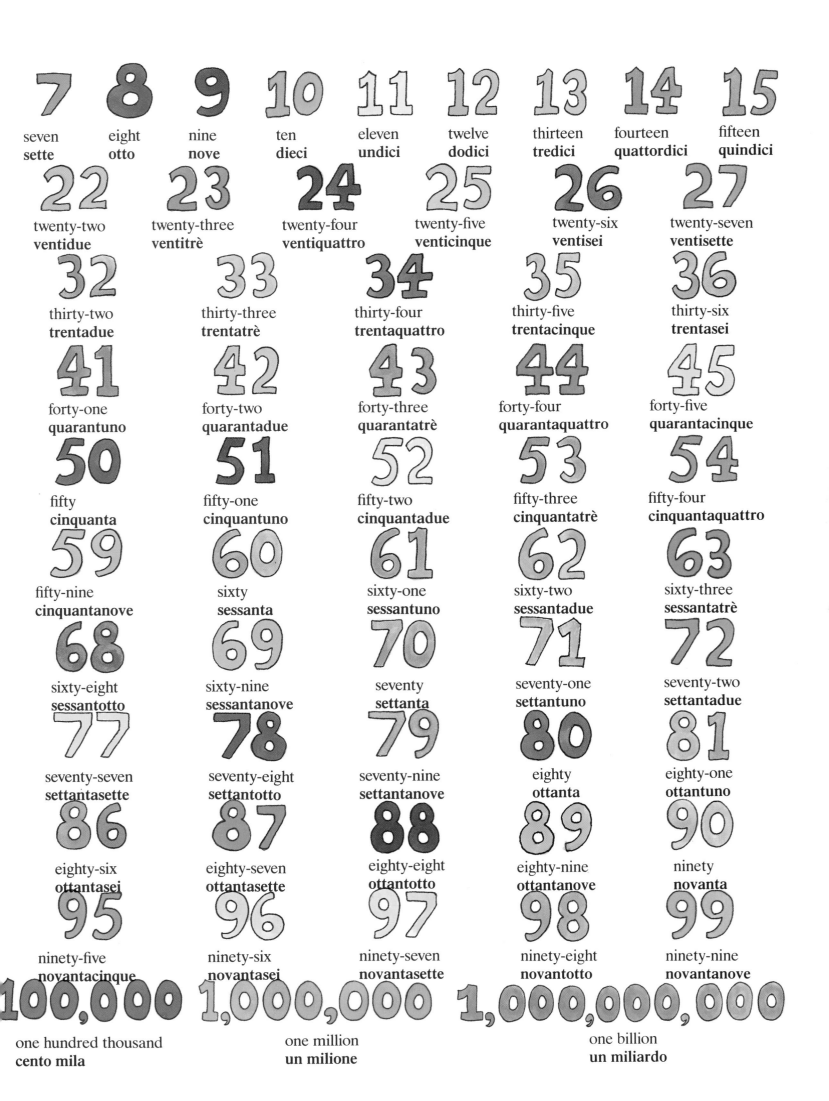

7 seven / sette

8 eight / otto

9 nine / nove

10 ten / dieci

11 eleven / undici

12 twelve / dodici

13 thirteen / tredici

14 fourteen / quattordici

15 fifteen / quindici

22 twenty-two / ventidue

23 twenty-three / ventitrè

24 twenty-four / ventiquattro

25 twenty-five / venticinque

26 twenty-six / ventisei

27 twenty-seven / ventisette

32 thirty-two / trentadue

33 thirty-three / trentatrè

34 thirty-four / trentaquattro

35 thirty-five / trentacinque

36 thirty-six / trentasei

41 forty-one / quarantuno

42 forty-two / quarantadue

43 forty-three / quarantatrè

44 forty-four / quarantaquattro

45 forty-five / quarantacinque

50 fifty / cinquanta

51 fifty-one / cinquantuno

52 fifty-two / cinquantadue

53 fifty-three / cinquantatrè

54 fifty-four / cinquantaquattro

59 fifty-nine / cinquantanove

60 sixty / sessanta

61 sixty-one / sessantuno

62 sixty-two / sessantadue

63 sixty-three / sessantatrè

68 sixty-eight / sessantotto

69 sixty-nine / sessantanove

70 seventy / settanta

71 seventy-one / settantuno

72 seventy-two / settantadue

77 seventy-seven / settantasette

78 seventy-eight / settantotto

79 seventy-nine / settantanove

80 eighty / ottanta

81 eighty-one / ottantuno

86 eighty-six / ottantasei

87 eighty-seven / ottantasette

88 eighty-eight / ottantotto

89 eighty-nine / ottantanove

90 ninety / novanta

95 ninety-five / novantacinque

96 ninety-six / novantasei

97 ninety-seven / novantasette

98 ninety-eight / novantotto

99 ninety-nine / novantanove

100,000 one hundred thousand / cento mila

1,000,000 one million / un milione

1,000,000,000 one billion / un miliardo

32. A Map of the World   La Carta Geografica del Mondo

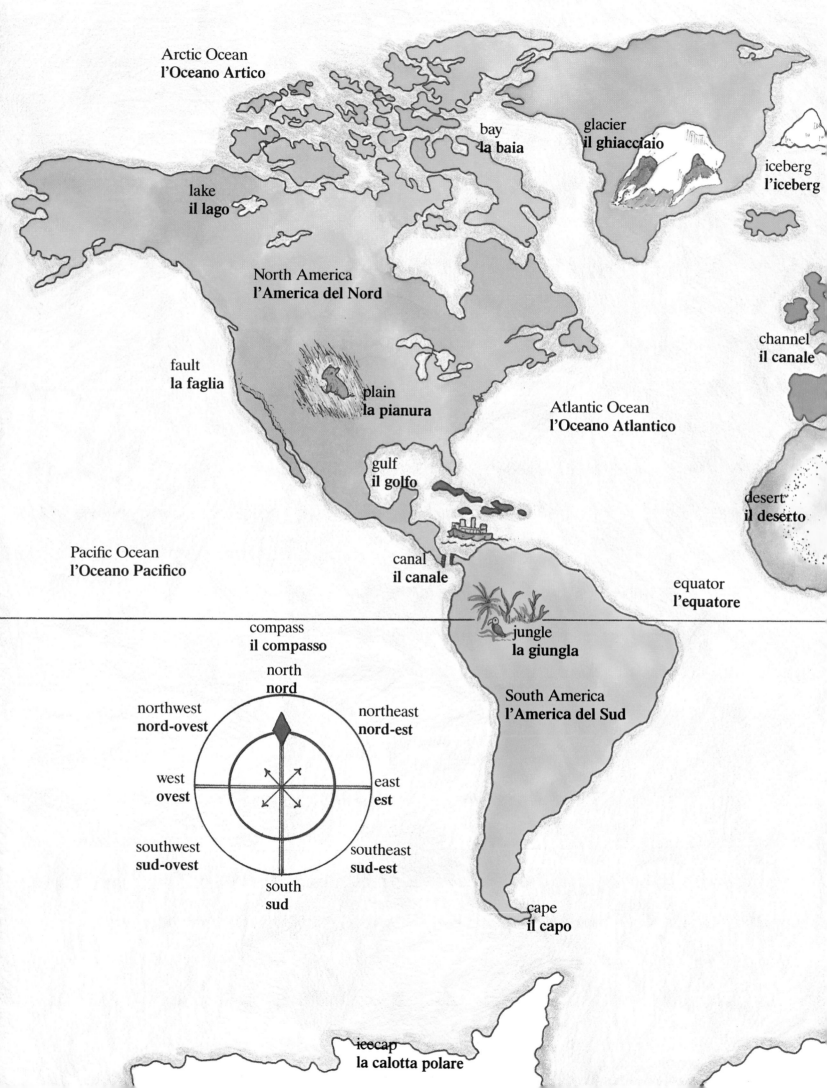

Arctic Ocean
l'Oceano Artico

bay
la baia

glacier
il ghiacciaio

iceberg
l'iceberg

lake
il lago

North America
l'America del Nord

channel
il canale

fault
la faglia

plain
la pianura

Atlantic Ocean
l'Oceano Atlantico

gulf
il golfo

desert
il deserto

Pacific Ocean
l'Oceano Pacifico

canal
il canale

equator
l'equatore

compass
il compasso

jungle
la giungla

north
nord

South America
l'America del Sud

northwest
nord-ovest

northeast
nord-est

west
ovest

east
est

southwest
sud-ovest

southeast
sud-est

south
sud

cape
il capo

icecap
la calotta polare

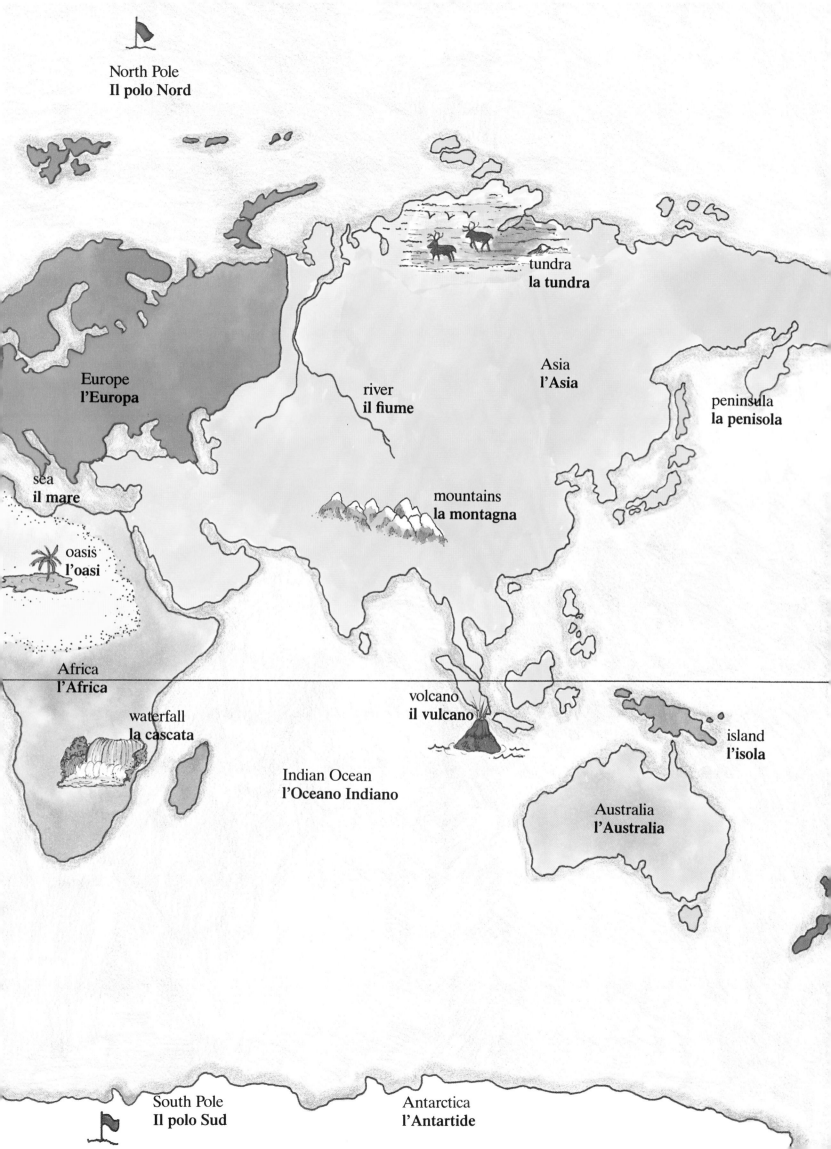

North Pole
Il polo Nord

tundra
la tundra

Asia
l'Asia

peninsula
la penisola

Europe
l'Europa

river
il fiume

sea
il mare

mountains
la montagna

oasis
l'oasi

Africa
l'Africa

volcano
il vulcano

island
l'isola

waterfall
la cascata

Indian Ocean
l'Oceano Indiano

Australia
l'Australia

South Pole
Il polo Sud

Antarctica
l'Antartide

Italian-English Glossary and Index

How to Say the Words in Italian

One of the most difficult things about learning a new language is pronunciation, how to say the words in the language. That's why we've written pronunciation guides to help you say the words in this book correctly. You will find a pronunciation guide in parentheses after each Italian word in the *Italian-English Glossary and Index*. It may look funny, but if you read it aloud, you will be saying the word correctly.

Here are a few hints about saying words in Italian. The Italian *r* is different from the English *r*. To say it correctly, "trill" the sound by flapping your tongue against the roof of your mouth. In Italian, the letter *a* always sounds like the *a* in f*a*ther, the letter *o* always sounds like the *o* in g*o*, and the letter *i* always sounds like the *ee* in f*ee*t. These sounds are written as *ah, oh,* and *ee* in the pronunciation guides. Also, the letter *e* sounds like the *ay* in pl*ay*. This sound is

written as *ay* in the pronunciation guides. Some combinations of letters also have special sounds in Italian. The combination *ai* sounds like the *i* in n*i*ght and is written as *igh* in the pronunciation guides. The combination *au* sounds like the *ow* in n*ow* and is written as *ow* in the pronunciation guides.

You may also notice that each word in the pronunciation guides has one syllable in heavy dark letters. This is the stressed syllable. When you say a word in English, you always say one syllable a little louder than the others. This is called the stressed syllable. When you read the pronunciation guides aloud, just say the syllables in heavy dark letters a little louder than the others to use the correct stress.

After the pronunciation guide, the *Italian-English Glossary and Index* gives the English meaning for each word and the number of the picture where you can find the word.

gli **abiti** (lyee **ah**-bee-tee), clothing, 7
l'**abito nero** (**lah**-bee-toh **nay**-roh), tuxedo, 4
l'**accappatoio** (lah-kahp-pah-**toy**-oh), bathrobe, 7
acceso (ah-**chay**-zoh), on, 26
l'**accetta** (lah-**chayt**-tah), ax, 25
l'**acqua** (**lah**-kwah), water, 24
l'**acquaio** (lah-**kwigh**-oh), sink, 3
l'**acquario** (lah-**kwah**-ree-oh), aquarium, 1
l'**acrobata** (lah-kroh-**bah**-tah), acrobat, 21
l'**aereo** (lah-**ay**-ray-oh), airplane, 16, 17
l'**aeroporto** (lah-ay-roh-**por**-toh), airport, 17
l'**Africa** (**lah**-free-kah), Africa, 32
l'**agente doganale** (lah-**jayn**-tay doh-gah-**nah**-lay), customs officer, 17
gli **aggettivi** (lyee ahj-jayt-**tee**-vee), adjectives, 26
aggiustare (ahj-joo-**stah**-ray), fix, 27
l'**aggraffatrice** (lahg-grahf-fah-**tree**-chay), stapler, 1
l'**agnello** (lahn-**yay**-loh), lamb, 9
l'**ago** (**lah**-goh), hypodermic needle, 11
l'**agricoltore** (lah-gree-kohl-**toh**-ray), farmer, 9
l'**aiuola** (ligh-oo-**oh**-lah), flowerbed, 5
l'**ala** (**lah**-lah), wing, 17
l'**alambicco** (lah-lahm-**beek**-koh), beaker, 23
l'**albergo** (lahl-**bayr**-goh), hotel, 8
l'**albero** (**lahl**-bay-roh), tree, 9, 24
l'**albero di famiglia** (**lahl**-bay-roh dee fah-**mee**-lyah), family tree, 29
l'**album di fotografie** (lahl-**boom** dee foh-toh-grah-**fee**-ay), photo album, 4
l'**alfabeto** (lahl-fah-**bay**-toh), alphabet, 1
l'**alga marina** (**lahl**-gah mah-**ree**-nah), seaweed, 22
le **ali** (lay **ah**-lee), wings, 20
l'**aliante** (lah-lee-**ahn**-tay), hang glider, 16
l'**altalena** (lahl-tah-**lay**-nah), swings, 8
alto (**ahl**-toh), tall, 26
l'**altoparlante** (lahl-toh-par-**lahn**-tay), loudspeaker, 1
l'**alunna** (lah-**loon**-nah), student (female), 1
l'**alunno** (lah-**loon**-noh), student (male), 1
alzarsi in piedi (al-**tsahr**-see een pee-**ay**-dee), stand up, 27
l'**amaca** (lah-**mah**-kah), hammock, 5
l'**America del Nord** (lah-**may**-ree-kah dayl nord), North America, 32
l'**America del Sud** (lah-**may**-ree-kah dayl sood), South America, 32

l'**amo** (**lah**-moh), fishhook, 22
l'**ananas** (lah-**nahn**-ahz), pineapple, 6
l'**anatroccolo** (lah-nah-**trohk**-koh-loh), duckling, 9
l'**ancora** (**lahn**-koh-rah), anchor, 22
andare (ahn-**dah**-ray), go, 27
andare a bicicletta (ahn-**dah**-ray ah bee-chee-**klayt**-tah), ride a bicycle, 27
l'**andare a vela** (lahn-**dah**-ray ah **vay**-lah), sailing, 18
l'**anello** (lah-**nayl**-loh), ring, 7
l'**angolo** (**lahn**-goh-loh), corner, 8
gli **animali** (lyee ah-nee-**mah**-lee), animals, 20
l'**anitra** (**lah**-nee-trah), duck, 9
l'**Antartide** (lahn-**tahr**-tee-day), Antarctica, 32
l'**antenna** (lahn-**tay**-nah), antenna, 23
l'**anticamera** (lahn-tee-**kah**-may-rah), waiting room, 11
aperto (ah-**payr**-toh), open, 26
le **api** (lay **ah**-pee), bees, 9
l'**apparecchio per denti** (lahp-pah-**ray**-kee-oh payr **dayn**-tee), braces, 11
aprire (ah-**pree**-ray), open, 27
l'**aquila** (**lah**-kwee-lah), eagle, 20
l'**aquilone** (lah-kwee-**loh**-nay), kite, 5
le **arachidi** (lay ah-**rah**-kee-dee), peanuts, 21
l'**aragosta** (lah-rah-**goh**-stah), lobster, 22
l'**arancia** (lah-**rahn**-chah), orange, 6
arancione (ah-rahn-**choh**-nay), orange, 28
l'**arbitro** (**lahr**-bee-troh), referee, umpire, 18
l'**archetto** (lahr-**kayt**-toh), bow, 19
l'**architetto** (lahr-kee-**tayt**-toh), architect, 15
l'**arciere** (lahr-**chay**-ray), archer, 25
l'**arco** (**lahr**-koh), bow, 25
l'**arcobaleno** (lahr-koh-bah-**lay**-noh), rainbow, 5
l'**arena** (lah-**ray**-nah), ring, 21
argenteo (ahr-**jayn**-tay-oh), silver, 28
l'**argento** (lahr-**jayn**-toh), silver, 22
l'**argilla** (lahr-**jeel**-lah), clay, 24
l'**armadietto farmaceutico** (lahr-mah-dee-**ayt**-toh fahr-mah-chay-**oo**-tee-koh), medicine cabinet, 2
l'**armadio a muro** (lahr-**mah**-dee-oh ah **moo**-roh), closet, 2
l'**arpa** (**lahr**-pah), harp, 19
l'**artiglio** (lahr-**tee**-lyoh), claws, 20
l'**artista** (lahr-**tee**-stah), artist, 15

l'**ascensore** (lah-shayn-**soh**-ray), elevator, 17
l'**asciugacapelli** (lah-shyoo-gah-kah-**pay**-lee), hair dryer, 12
l'**asciugamani di carta** (lah-shyoo-gah-**mah**-nee dee **kahr**-tah), paper towels, 3
l'**asciugamano** (lah-shyoo-gah-**mah**-noh), towel, 2
l'**asciugatrice** (lah-shyoo-gah-**tree**-chay), clothes dryer, 3
ascoltare (ah-skohl-**tah**-ray), listen (to), 27
l'**Asia** (**lah**-zee-ah), Asia, 32
l'**asino** (**lah**-zee-noh), donkey, 9
aspetta (ah-**spayt**-tah), wait!, 16
aspettare (ah-spayt-**tah**-ray), wait, 27
l'**aspirapolvere** (lah-spee-rah-**pohl**-vay-ray), vacuum cleaner, 3
l'**assegno** (lahs-**say**-nyoh), check, 13
l'**assistente del dentista** (lahs-see-**stayn**-tay dayl dayn-**tee**-stah), dental hygienist, 11
l'**assistente del medico** (lahs-see-**stayn**-tay dayl **may**-dee-koh), paramedic, 15
l'**assistente di volo** (lahs-see-**stayn**-tay dee **voh**-loh), flight attendant, 17
l'**asta della tenda** (**lah**-stah **dayl**-lah **tayn**-dah), tent pole, 21
l'**asteroide** (lah-stay-**roy**-day), asteroid, 23
l'**astronauta** (lah-stroh-**now**-tah), astronaut, 23
l'**astronave** (lah-stroh-**nah**-vay), spaceship, 23
l'**astronomo** (lah-**stroh**-noh-moh), astronomer, 15
l'**atleta** (laht-**lay**-tah), athlete, 15
l'**attaccapanni** (laht-tahk-kah-**pahn**-nee), hanger, 2
le **attività** (lay aht-tee-vee-**tah**), actions, 27
l'**attore** (laht-**toh**-ray), actor, 19
l'**attrezzo ginnico** (laht-**tray**-tsoh **jeen**-nee-koh), jungle gym, 8
l'**attrice** (laht-**tree**-chay), actress, 19
l'**auditorio** (low-dee-**toh**-ree-oh), auditorium, 19
l'**Australia** (low-**strah**-lee-ah), Australia, 32
l'**autobus** (**low**-toh-boos), bus, 16
l'**autobus per scuola** (**low**-toh-boos payr **skwoh**-lah), school bus, 16
l'**autocisterna** (low-toh-chee-**stayr**-nah), tank truck, 14
l'**autolavaggio** (low-toh-lah-**vahj**-joh), car wash, 14

l'autopompa (low-toh-**pohm**-pah), fire engine, 16

l'autorespiratore (low-toh-ray-spee-rah-**toh**-ray), oxygen tank, 22

l'autunno (low-**toon**-noh), fall, 5

avanti (ah-**vahn**-tee), go!, 16

l'aviorimessa (lah-vee-oh-ree-**mays**-sah), hangar, 17

l'avocado (lah-voh-**kah**-doh), avocado, 6

l'avvocatessa (lahv-voh-kah-**tays**-sah), lawyer, 15

il babbo (eel **bahb**-boh), dad, 29

la bacchetta magica (lah bahk-**kayt**-tah **mah**-jee-kah), magic wand, 25

la bacheca (lah bah-**kay**-kah), bulletin board, 1

i baffi (ee **bahf**-fee), mustache, 12

bagnarsi (bah-**nyahr**-see), take a bath, 27

la baia (la **bigh**-ah), bay, 32

il balcone (eel bahl-**koh**-nay), balcony, 8

la balena (lah bah-**lay**-nah), whale, 22

ballare (bahl-**lah**-ray), dance, 27

la ballerina (lah bahl-lay-**ree**-nah), dancer, 19

la bambola (lah **bahm**-boh-lah), doll, 4

la banana (lah bah-**nah**-nah), banana, 6

la banca (lah **bahn**-kah), bank, 13

il banchiere (eel bahn-**kyay**-ray), banker, 15

il banco (eel **bahn**-koh), counter, 3; pupil desk, 1; school (of fish), 22

il banco corallifero (eel **bahn**-koh koh-rahl-**lee**-fay-roh), coral reef, 22

il bancomat (eel **bahn**-koh-maht), automatic teller, 13

la banda (lah **bahn**-dah), band, 21

le bandiere (lay bahn-**dyay**-ray), flags, 17

la barba (lah **bahr**-bah), beard, 12

il barbiere (eel bahr-**byay**-ray), barber, 12

dal barbiere (dahl bahr-**byay**-ray), barber shop, 12

la barca a remi (lah **bahr**-kah ah **ray**-mee), rowboat, 16

la barca a vela (lah **bahr**-kah ah **vay**-lah), sailboat, 16

la barca (lah **bahr**-kah), boat, 16

il baseball (eel **bah**-zay-bahl), baseball, 18

basso (**bahs**-soh), short, 26

il bastoncino (eel bah-stohn-**chee**-noh), stick, 24

il bastone (eel bah-**stoh**-nay), cane, 11; club, 24

il battone (eel baht-**toh**-nay), baton, 21

il baule (eel **bow**-lay), trunk, 4

la bavella (lah bah-**vayl**-lah), dental floss, 11

il becco (eel **bayk**-koh), beak, 20

il bendaggio a fionda (eel bayn-**dahj**-joh ah fee-**ohn**-dah), sling, 11

bere (**bay**-ray), drink, 27

la betoniera (lah bay-tohn-ee-**ay**-rah), cement mixer, 16

la bevanda (lah bay-**vahn**-dah), soft drink, 10

la biancheria intima (lah bee-ahn-kay-**ree**-ah **een**-tee-mah), underwear, 7

bianco (bee-**ahn**-koh), white, 28

il bibliotecario (eel beeb-lee-oh-tay-**kah**-ree-oh), librarian, 15

il bicchiere (eel beek-kee-**ay**-ray), glass, 10

la bicicletta (lah bee-chee-**klayt**-tah), bicycle, 14, 16, 18

il bigliettaio (eel beel-yay-**tigh**-oh), ticket agent, 17

la biglietteria (lah beel-yayt-tay-**ree**-ah), ticket booth, 21

i biglietti (eel beel-**yayt**-tee), tickets, 21

il biglietto (eel beel-**yayt**-toh), bill, 13; ticket, 17

i bigodini (ee bee-goh-**dee**-nee), curlers, 12

la bilancia (lah bee-**lahn**-chah), scale, 6, 13

il binocolo (eel bee-**noh**-koh-loh), binoculars, 17

biondi (bee-**ohn**-dee), blond, 12

i biscotti (ee bee-**skoht**-tee), cookies, 6

il bisonte (eel bee-**zohn**-tay), bison, 24

la bistecca (lah bee-**stayk**-kah), steak, 10

i blocchi (ee **bloh**-kee), blocks, 4

il blocco (eel **blohk**-koh), notepad, 13

blu (bloo), blue, 28

la bocca di accesso (lah **bohk**-kah dee ah-**chays**-soh), manhole cover, 8

la bocca (lah **boh**-kah), mouth, 11

il boccaglio (eel bohk-**kahl**-yoh), snorkel, 22

il bollitore (eel bohl-lee-**toh**-ray), kettle, 3

la borsa (lah **bohr**-sah), purse, 17

la borsa per documenti (lah **bohr**-sah payr doh-koo-**mayn**-tee), briefcase, 17

la bottiglia (lah boht-**teel**-yah), bottle, 6

il bottone (eel boht-**toh**-nay), button, 7

il braccialetto (eel brah-chah-**layt**-toh), bracelet, 7

il braccio (eel **brah**-choh), arm, 11

le branchie (lay **brahn**-kee-ay), gills, 22

le briglie (lay **breel**-yay), reins, 25

i broccoletti (ee brohk-koh-**layt**-tee), broccoli, 10

la buca dell'orchestra (lah **boo**-kah dayl-lohr-**kay**-strah), orchestra pit, 19

il bucato (eel boo-**kah**-toh), laundry, 3

il buco delle lettere (eel **boo**-koh **dayl**-lay layt-**tay**-ray), mail slot, 13

buono (boo-**oh**-noh), good, 26

il burlone (eel boor-**loh**-nay), court jester, 25

il burrattino (eel boor-raht-**tee**-noh), puppet, 4

il burro (eel **boor**-roh), butter, 6

la cabina telefonica (lah kah-**bee**-nah tay-lay-**foh**-nee-kah), phone booth, 13

la caccia (lah **kah**-chah), hunt, 26

il cacciatore (eel kah-chah-**toh**-ray), hunter, 24

il cacciavite (eel kah-chah-**vee**-tay), screwdriver, 3

il cactus (eel **kahk**-toos), cactus, 1

cadere (kah-**day**-ray), fall, 27

il caffè (eel kahf-**fay**), coffee, 10

il calamaro (eel kah-lah-**mah**-roh), squid, 22

il calcio (eel **kahl**-choh), soccer, 18

il calcolatore (eel kahl-koh-lah-**toh**-ray), calculator, 1

caldo (**kahl**-doh), hot, 26

il calendario (eel kah-layn-**dah**-ree-oh), calendar, 1

la calotta polare (lah kah-**loht**-tah poh-**lah**-ray), icecap, 32

calvo (**kahl**-voh), bald, 12

la calzamaglia (lah kahl-tsah-**mahl**-yah), leotard, 19; tights, 7

i calzini (ee kahl-**tsee**-nee), socks, 7

i calzoncini corti (ee kahl-tsohn-**chee**-nee **kohr**-tee), shorts, 7

la camera da letto (lah **kah**-may-rah dah **layt**-toh), bedroom, 2

la cameriera (lah kah-may-ree-**ay**-rah), waitress, 10

il cameriere (eel kah-may-ree-**ay**-ray), waiter, 10

il camerino (eel kah-may-**ree**-noh), dressing room, 19

il camice (eel kah-**mee**-chay), lab coat, 23

la camicetta (lah kah-mee-**chayt**-tah), blouse, 7

la camicia (lah kah-**mee**-chah), shirt, 7

il camino (eel kah-**mee**-noh), chimney, 2

il camion (eel kah-mee-**ohn**), truck, 16

il camionista (eel kah-mee-oh-**nee**-stah), truck driver, 14

il cammello (eel kahm-**mayl**-loh), camel, 20

camminare (kahm-mee-**nah**-ray), walk, 27

la campanella (lah kahm-pah-**nayl**-lah), bell, 1

il camper (eel **kahm**-payr), camper, 16

il campo (eel **kahm**-poh), field, 24

il canale (eel kah-**nah**-lay), canal, 32; channel, 32

il cancellino (eel kahn-chayl-**lee**-noh), eraser (chalkboard), 1

la candela (lah kahn-**day**-lah), candle, 10

il cane (eel **kah**-nay), dog, 9

il canguro (eel kahn-**goo**-roh), kangaroo, 20

il cannone (eel kahn-**noh**-nay), cannon, 22

la cannuccia (lah kahn-**noo**-chah), straw, 10

la canoa (lah kah-**noh**-ah), canoe, 16

il cantante (eel kahn-**tahn**-tay), singer, 19

cantare (kahn-**tah**-ray), sing, 27

la capanna (lah kah-**pahn**-nah), hut, 24

i capelli (ee kah-**payl**-lee), hair, 12

il capo (eel **kah**-poh), cape, 32

il capomastro (eel kah-poh-**mah**-stroh), foreman, 15

il cappello (eel kahp-**payl**-loh), hat, 4, 7

il cappello a cilindro (eel kahp-**payl**-loh ah chee-**leen**-droh), top hat, 4

il cappello da sci (eel kahp-**payl**-loh dah shee), cap, 7

il cappello di cowboy (eel kahp-**payl**-loh dee **kow**-boy), cowboy hat, 4

il cappotto (eel kahp-**poht**-toh), coat, 7

il cappuccio (eel kahp-**poo**-choh), hood, 7

la capra (lah **kah**-prah), goat, 9

il capretto (eel kah-**prayt**-toh), kid, 9

la capsula spaziale (lah **kahp**-soo-lah spah-tsee-**ah**-lay), landing capsule, 23

le caramelle (lay kah-rah-**mayl**-lay), candy, 6

il carcere (eel **kahr**-chay-ray), jail, 8

il carcere sotterraneo (eel **kahr**-chay-ray soht-tayr-**rah**-nay-oh), dungeon, 25

la carne (lah **kahr**-nay), meat, 6

le carote (lay kah-**roh**-tay), carrots, 6

il carrello (eel kahr-**rayl**-loh), shopping cart, 6

il carrello d'atterraggio (eel kahr-**rayl**-loh daht-tayr-**rahj**-joh), landing gear, 17

il carrello per bagagli (eel kahr-**rayl**-loh payr bah-gah-lyee), baggage cart, 17

il carro (eel **kahr**-roh), cart, 24

il carro attrezzi (eel **kahr**-roh aht-**tray**-tsee), tow truck, 14

la carrozzina (lah kahr-roh-**tsee**-nah), baby carriage, 16

la carta (lah **kahr**-tah), paper, 1

la carta di credito (lah **kahr**-tah dee **kray**-dee-toh), credit card, 13

la carta geografica (lah **kahr**-tah jay-oh-**grah**-fee-kah), map, 1

la carta igienica (lah **kahr**-tah ee-**jay**-nee-kah), toilet paper, 2

la carta vetrata (lah **kahr**-tah **vay**-trah-tah), sandpaper, 3

le carte (lay **kahr**-tay), cards, 4

le carte di musica (lay **kahr**-tay dee **moo**-zee-kah), sheet music, 19

il cartellino (eel kahr-tayl-**lee**-noh), sign, 6

il cartellone (el kahr-tayl-**loh**-nay), poster, 2

la cartolina (lah kahr-**toh**-lee-nah), postcard, 13

la casa da bambole (lah **kah**-zah dah **bahm**-boh-lay), dollhouse, 4

la casa (lah **kah**-zah), house, 2

la cascata (lah kah-**skah**-tah), waterfall, 32

la cassa (lah **kahs**-sah), cash register, 6

la cassaforte (lah kahs-sah-**fohr**-tay), safe, 13

il cassetone (eel kahs-say-**toh**-nay), treasure chest, 22

la cassetta (lah kahs-**sayt**-tah), cassette tape, 2

la cassetta di sicurezza (lah kahs-**sayt**-tah dee see-koo-**ray**- tsah), safety deposit box, 13

la cassetta per imbucare (lah kahs-**sayt**-tah payr eem-boo-**kah**- ray), post-office box, 13

la cassetta postale (lah kahs-**sayt**-tah poh-**stah**-lay), mailbox, 13

il cassettino (eel kahs-sayt-**tee**-noh), drawer, 3

la cassiere (lah kahs-see-**ay**-ray), cashier, 6

il cassiere (eel kahs-see-**ay**-ray), teller, 13

castagni (kah-**stan**-yee), brown, 12

il castello (eel kah-**stayl**-loh), castle, 25

la catena (lah kah-**tay**-nah), bicycle chain, 14

la cattedra (lah kaht-**tay**-drah), teacher's desk, 1

il cavaliere (eel kah-vahl-**yay**-ray), knight, 25

la cavallerizza senza sella (lah kah-vahl-lay-**ree**-tsah **sayn**-tsah **sayl**-lah), bareback rider, 21

la cavalletta (lah kah-vahl-**layt**-tah), grasshopper, 5

il cavalletto (eel kah-vahl-**layt**-toh), easel, 1; kickstand, 14

il cavallo (eel kah-**vahl**-loh), horse, 9

il cavallo a dondolo (eel kah-**vahl**-loh ah **dohn**-doh-loh), rocking horse, 4

il cavallo di mare (eel kah-**vahl**-loh dee **mah**-ray), sea horse, 22

la caverna (lah kah-**vayr**-nah), cave, 24

i cavernicoli (ee Kah-vayr-**nee**-koh-lee), cave dwellers, 24

la caviglia (lah kah-**vee**-lyah), ankle, 11

il cavolo (eel **kah**-voh-loh), cabbage, 6

il cellofan (eel chayl-loh-**fahn**), **cellophane tape, 1**

la cena (lah **chay**-nah), dinner, 10

il cencio (eel **chayn**-choh), rag, 14

cento (**chayn**-toh), hundred, 31

cento mila (**chayn**-toh **mee**-lah), hundred thousand, 31

il ceppo (eel **chayp**-poh), log, 5

cercare (chayr-**kah**-ray), look for, 27

il cerchio (eel **chayr**-kee-oh), hoop, 21

i cereali (ee chay-ray-**ah**-lee), cereal, 6

il cerimoniere (eel chay-ree-moh-nee-**ay**-ray), master of ceremonies, 19

la cerniera (lay chayr-nee-**ay**-rah), zipper, 7

il cerotto medicato (eel chay-**roht**-toh may-dee-**kah**-toh), bandage, 11

il cervo (eel **chayr**-voh), deer, 20

il cespuglio (eel chay-**spool**-yoh), bush, 5

la cesta (lah **chay**-stah), basket, 24

il cestino (eel chay-**stee**-noh), wastebasket, 1

il chiappamosche (eel kee-ahp-pah-**moh**-skay), fly swatter, 5

chiaro (kee-**ah**-roh), light, 26

la chiave (lah kee-**ah**-vay), key, 13; wrench, 3

la chiesa (lah kee-**ay**-zah), church, 8

il chignon (eel keen-**yohn**), bun, 12

il chiodo (eel kee-**oh**-doh), nail, 3

la chitarra (lah kee-**tahr**-rah), guitar, 19

chiudere (**kyoo**-day-ray), close, 27

chiuso (**kyoo**-zoh), closed, 26

il cibo (eel **chee**-boh), food, 6

il ciclismo (eel chee-**klee**-zmoh), cycling, 18

il cielo (eel chee-**ay**-loh), sky, 9

il cigno (eel **cheen**-yoh), swan, 20

le ciliege (lay chee-lee-**ay**-jay), cherries, 6

il cilindro (eel chee-**leen**-droh), cylinder, 30

la cima (lah **chee**-mah), top, 26

il cinema (eel **chee**-nay-mah), movie theatre, 8

cinquanta (cheen-**kwahn**-tah), fifty, 31

cinquantacinque (cheen-kwahn-tah-**cheen**-kway), fifty-five, 31

cinquantadue (cheen-kwahn-tah-**doo**-ay), fifty-two, 31

cinquantanove (cheen-kwahn-tah-**noh**-vay), fifty-nine, 31

cinquantaquattro (cheen-kwahn-tah-**kwaht**-troh), fifty-four, 31

cinquantasei (cheen-kwahn-tah-**say**-ee), fifty-six, 31

cinquantasette (cheen-kwahn-tah-**sayt**-tay), fifty-seven, 31

cinquantatrè (cheen-kwahn-tah-**tray**), fifty-three, 31

cinquantotto (cheen-kwahn-**toht**-toh), fifty-eight, 31

cinquantuno (cheen-kwahn-**too**-noh), fifty-one, 31

cinque (**cheen**-kway), five, 31

la cintura (lah cheen-**too**-rah), belt, 7

la cintura di sicurezza (lah cheen-**too**-rah dee see-koo-**ray**-tsah), seat belt, 14

la cioccolata (lah choh-koh-**lah**-tah), chocolate, 6

le cipolle (lay chee-**pohl**-lay), onions, 6

la cipra (lah **chee**-prah), powder, 12

il circo (eel **cheer**-koh), circus, 21

i circoli (ee **cheer**-koh-lee), rings, 23

il circolo (eel **cheer**-koh-loh), circle, 30

la città (lah cheet-**tah**), city, 8

il clarinetto (eel klah-ree-**nayt**-toh), clarinet, 19

la classe (lah **klahs**-say), classroom, 1

il coccodrillo (eel kohk-koh-**dreel**-loh), alligator, 20

il cocomero (eel koh-koh-**may**-roh), watermelon, 6

la coda (lah **koh**-dah), tail, 20

la coda di cavallo (lah **koh**-dah dee kah-**vahl**-loh), ponytail, 12

il codice postale (eel **koh**-dee-chay poh-**stah**-lay), zip code, 13

il cofano (eel **koh**-fah-noh), hood, 14

la colazione (lah koh-lah-tsee-**oh**-nay), breakfast, 10

la colla (lah **kohl**-lah), glue, 1

la collana (lah kohl-**lah**-nah), necklace, 7

la collina (lah kohl-**lee**-nah), hill, 9

il collo (eel **kohl**-loh), collar, 7

il colore (eel koh-**loh**-ray), paint, 1, 24

colori (koh-**loh**-ree), colors, 28

il coltello (eel kohl-**tayl**-loh), knife, 10

la cometa (lah koh-**may**-tah), comet, 23

la commessa (lah kohm-**mays**-sah), saleswoman, 15

il commesso (eel kohm-**mays**-soh), salesman, 15

la communità (lah kohm-moo-nee-**tah**), community, 15

il compact disc (eel kohm-**pahkt** deesk), compact disc, 2

il compasso (eel kohm-**pahs**-soh), compass, 1, 32

il completo (eel kohm-**play**-toh), suit, 7

comprare (kohm-**prah**-ray), buy, 27

il computer (eel kohm-**poo**-tayr), computer, 23

la conchiglia (lah kohn-**keel**-yah), seashell, 22

il Concorde (eel kohn-**kohr**-day), Concorde, 17

il congelatore (eel kohn-jay-lah-**toh**-ray), freezer, 3

il coniglio (eel koh-**neel**-yoh), rabbit, 9

il cono (eel **koh**-noh), cone, 30

il controllore di volo (eel kohn-trohl-**loh**-ray dee **voh**-loh), air-traffic controller, 17

il coperchio del serbatoio (eel koh-**payr**-kee-oh dayl sayr-bah-**toy**-oh), gas cap, 14

la coperta di lana (lah koh-**payr**-tah dee **lah**-nah), blanket, 2

il copione (eel koh-pee-**oh**-nay), script, 19

il coprimozzo (eel koh-pree-**moh**-tsoh), hubcap, 14

il corallo (eel koh-**rahl**-loh), coral, 22

la corazza (lah koh-**rah**-tsah), armor, 25

la corda (lah **kohr**-dah), jump rope, 4; rope, 19, 21; strings, 19

la corda tesa per funamboli (lah **kohr**-dah **tay**-zah payr foo-**nahm**-boh-lee), tightrope, 21

le corna (lay **kohr**-nah), horns, 9, 20

il cornetto (eel kohr-**nayt**-toh), French horn, 19

la cornice (lah **kohr**-nee-chay), picture frame, 4

la corona (lah koh-**roh**-nah), crown, 25

correre (**kohr**-ray-ray), run, 27

il correre (eel **kohr**-ray-ray), running, 18

la corsa (lah **kohr**-sah), car racing, 18

la corsa a ostacoli (lah **kohr**-sah ah oh-**stah**-koh-lee), hurdles, 18

la corsa da cavalli (lah **kohr**-sah dah kah-**vahl**-lee), horse racing, 18

corti (**kohr**-tee), short, 12

il cortile (eel kohr-**tee**-lay), courtyard, 25; yard, 5

corto (**kohr**-toh), short, 26

la costellazione (lah koh-stayl-lah-tsee-**oh**-nay), constellation, 23

il costume (eel koh-**stoo**-may), costume, 19

il costume da bagno (eel koh-**stoo**-may dah **bah**-nyoh), bathing suit, 7

il cowboy (eel **kow**-boy), cowboy, 15

i crackers (ee **krah**-kayrs), crackers, 6

il cratere (eel krah-**tay**-ray), crater, 23

la cravatta (lah krah-**vaht**-tah), tie, 7

la crema da barba (lah **kray**-mah dah **bahr**-bah), shaving cream, 12

il cricco (eel **kreek**-koh), jack, 14

la criniera (lah kree-nee-**ay**-rah), mane, 20

il cristallo di luna (eel kree-**stahl**-loh dee **loo**-nah), moon rock, 23

il cronista (eel kroh-**nee**-stah), reporter, 15

il crostino (eel kroh-**stee**-noh), toast, 10

il cruscotto (eel kroo-**skoht**-toh), dashboard, 14

il cubo (eel **koo**-boh), cube, 30

il cucchiaio (eel kook-kee-**igh**-oh), spoon, 10

il cucciolo (eel koo-**choh**-loh), puppy, 9

la cucina (lah koo-**chee**-nah), kitchen, 2, 3

cucinare (koo-chee-**nah**-ray), cook, 27

la cuffia (lah **koof**-fee-ah), headset, 17

la cugina (lah koo-**jee**-nah), cousin (female), 29

il cugino (eel koo-**jee**-noh), cousin (male), 29

la culla (lah **kool**-lah), cradle, 4

il cuoco (eel koo-**oh**-koh), cook, 15

il cuoio (eel koo-**oy**-oh), leather, 24

i dadi (ee **dah**-dee), dice, 4

dare (**dah**-ray), give, 27

dare un calcio (**dah**-ray oon **kahl**-choh), kick, 27

davanti (dah-**vahn**-tee), in front of, 26

decimo (**day**-chee-moh), tenth, 31

il delfino (eel dayl-**fee**-noh), dolphin, 22

il denaro (eel day-**nahr**-oh), money, 6

il dente (eel **dayn**-tay), tooth, 11

il dentifricio (eel dayn-tee-**free**-choh), toothpaste, 11

il dentista (eel dayn-**tee**-stah), dentist, 11

dal dentista (dahl dayn-**tee**-stah), dentist's office, 11

il deposito bagagli (eel day-**poh**-zee-toh bah-**gahl**-yee), luggage compartment, 17

il deserto (eel day-**zayr**-toh), desert, 32

destro (**day**-stroh), right, 26

il detersivo (eel day-tayr-**see**-voh), laundry detergent, 3

diciannove (dee-chah-**noh**-vay), nineteen, 31

diciasette (dee-chah-**sayt**-tay), seventeen, 31

diciotto (dee-**choht**-toh), eighteen, 31

dieci mila (dee-**ay**-chee **mee**-lah), ten thousand, 31

dieci (dee-**ay**-chee), ten, 31

dietro (dee-**ay**-troh), behind, 26

difficile (dee-fee-**chee**-lay), difficult, 26

il dinosauro (eel dee-noh-**zow**-roh), dinosaur, 24

dipingere (dee-**peen**-jay-ray), paint, 27

il direttore d'orchestra (eel dee-rayt-**toh**-ray dohr-**kay**-strah), conductor, 19

il dirigibile (eel dee-ree-**jee**-bee-lay), blimp, 16

il disc jockey (eel deesk **joh**-kee), disc jockey, 15

il disco (eel **dee**-skoh), record, 2

disegnare (dee-zay-**nyah**-ray), draw, 27

il disegno di caverna (eel dee-**zay**-nyoh dee kah-**vayr**-nah), cave drawing, 24

il dito (eel **dee**-toh), finger, 11

il dito del piede (eel **dee**-toh dayl pee-**ay**-day), toe, 11

il divano (eel dee-**vah**-noh), sofa, 2

la divisa (lah dee-**vee**-zah), uniform, 4

la doccia (lah **doh**-chah), shower, 2

dodici (**doh**-dee-chee), twelve, 31

il domatore dei leoni (eel doh-mah-**toh**-ray day-ee lay-**oh**-nee), lion tamer, 21

la donna (lah **dohn**-nah), woman, 9

la donna poliziotto (lah **dohn**-nah poh-lee-tsee-**oht**-toh), policewoman, 15

dorato (doh-**rah**-toh), gold, 28

dormire (dohr-**mee**-ray), sleep, 27

la dottoressa (lah doht-toh-**rays**-sah), doctor, 11

il drago (eel **drah**-goh), dragon, 25

la drogheria (lah droh-gay-**ree**-ah), grocery store, 8

due (**doo**-ay), two, 31

duro (**doo**-roh), hard, 26

l'edificio (lay-dee-**fee**-choh), building, 8

l'edificio degli appartamenti (lay-dee-**fee**-choh **dayl**-yee ahp-pahr-tah-**mayn**-tee), apartment building, 8

l'elastico (lay-**lah**-stee-koh), rubber band, 13

l'elefante (lay-lay-**fahn**-tay), elephant, 20, 21

l'elettricista (lay-layt-tree-**chee**-stah), electrician, 15

l'elfo (**layl**-foh), elf, 25

l'elica (**lay**-lee-kah), propeller, 17

l'elicottero (lay-lee-**koht**-tay-roh), helicopter, 16

l'elmetto (layl-**may**-toh), helmet, 18

l'elmo (**layl**-moh), helm, 22

l'elmo spaziale (**layl**-moh spah-tsee-**ah**-lay), space helmet, 23

l'equatore (lay-kwah-**toh**-ray), equator, 32

l'equitazione (lay-kwee-tah-tsee-**oh**-nay), horseback riding, 18

l'erba (**layr**-bah), grass, 9

est (ayst), east, 32

l'estate (lay-**stah**-tay), summer, 5

l'etichetta (lay-tee-**kayt**-tah), label, 13

l'Europa (lay-oo-**roh**-pah), Europe, 32

l'extraterreste (lay-strah-tayr-**ray**-stay), alien, 23

la fabbrica (lah **fahb**-bree-kah), factory, 8

il fabbro ferraio (eel **fahb**-broh fayr-**righ**-oh), blacksmith, 25

il facchino (eel fahk-**kee**-noh), porter, 17

la faccia (lah **fah**-chah), face, 11

facile (**fah**-chee-lay), easy, 26

i fagiolini (ee fah-joh-**lee**-nee), green beans, 6

la faglia (lah **fahl**-yah), fault, 32

la falciatrice meccanica (lah fahl-chah-**tree**-chay mak-**kah**-nee- kah), lawn mower, 5

il falegname (eel fah-lay-**nyah**-may), carpenter, 15

il fanalo (eel fah-**nah**-loh), headlight, 14

il fango (eel **fahn**-goh), mud, 5

fare giochi (**fah**-ray **joh**-kee), juggle, 27

la faretra (lah fah-**ray**-trah), quiver, 25

la farfalla (lah fahr-**fahl**-lah), butterfly, 5

la farina (lah fah-**ree**-nah), flour, 3

la farmacia (lah fahr-mah-**chee**-ah), drugstore, pharmacy, 8

la farmacista (lah fahr-mah-**chee**-stah), pharmacist, 15

il faro (eel **fah**-roh), lighthouse, 16

il fascio di luce (eel **fah**-shoh dee **loo**-chay), spotlight, 19

la fattoria (lah faht-toh-**ree**-ah), farm, 9

il fazzoletto (eel fah-tsoh-**layt**-toh), handkerchief, 7

la felce (lah **fayl**-chay), fern, 24

felice (fay-**lee**-chay), happy, 26

il fenicottero (eel fay-nee-**koht**-tay-roh), flamingo, 20

il fermacapelli (eel fayr-mah-kah-**payl**-lee), barrette, 12

la fermata (lah fayr-**mah**-tah), bus stop, 16

i ferri da calza (ee **fayr**-ree dah **kahl**-tsah), knitting needles, 4

il ferro da stiro (eel **fayr**-roh dah **stee**-roh), iron, 3

il ferro di cavallo (eel **fayr**-roh dee kah-**vahl**-loh), horseshoe, 25

il ferro per arricciare i capelli (eel **fayr**-roh payr ahr-ree-**chah**-ray ee kah-**payl**-lee), curling iron, 12

la festa di compleanno (lah **fay**-stah dee kohm-play-**ahn**-noh), birthday party, 10

i fiammiferi (ee fee-ahm-**mee**-fay-ree), matches, 5

la fibbia (lah **feeb**-bee-ah), buckle, 7

il fieno (eel fee-**ay**-noh), hay, 9

la figlia (lah **feel**-yah), daughter, 29

il figlio (eel **feel**-yoh), son, 29

la filaccia (lah fee-**lah**-chah), yarn, 4

il filatoio (eel fee-lah-**toy**-oh), spinning wheel, 4

la finestra (lah fee-**nay**-strah), window, 2

il fiocco (eel fee-**ohk**-koh), bow, 13

il fiocco di neve (eel fee-**ohk**-koh dee **nay**-vay), snowflake, 5

i fiori (ee fee-**oh**-ree), flowers, 5

la fiorista (lah fee-oh-**ree**-stah), florist, 15

la firma (lah **feer**-mah), signature, 13

la fisarmonica (lah fee-zahr-**moh**-nee-kah), accordion, 19

il fiume (eel fee-**oo**-may), river, 32

il flauto (eel **flow**-toh), flute, 19

la foca (lah **foh**-kah), seal, 20

il focolare (eel foh-koh-**lah**-ray), fireplace, 2

la foglia (lah **fohl**-yah), leaf, 5

il fon (eel fohn), blow dryer, 12

il fondo (eel **fohn**-doh), bottom, 26; cross-country skiing, 18

la fontana (lah fohn-**tah**-nah), fountain, 8

il food processor (eel food processor), food processor, 3

il football americano (eel **foot**-bahl ah-may-ree-**kah**-noh), football, 18

il footing (eel **foo**-teeng), jogging, 18

le forbici (lay **fohr**-bee-chee), scissors, 1, 12

la forchetta (lah fohr-**kayt**-tah), fork, 10

la foresta (lah foh-**ray**-stah), forest, 25

il formaggio (eel fohr-**mahj**-joh), cheese, 6

le forme (lay **fohr**-may), shapes, 30

la formica (lah fohr-**mee**-kah), ant, 9

la fornace (lah fohr-**nah**-chay), forge, 25; kiln, 24

il fornello (eel fohr-**nayl**-loh), stove, 3

il forno (eel **fohr**-noh), oven, 3

il forno a microonda (eel **fohr**-noh ah mee-kroh-**ohn**-dah), microwave oven, 3

il fosso (eel **fohs**-soh), moat, 25

la foto (lah **foh**-toh), photograph, 4

il fotografo (eel foh-toh-**grah**-foh), photographer, 15

le fragole (lay **frah**-goh-lay), strawberries, 6

il francobollo (eel frahn-koh-**bohl**-loh), stamp, 13

la frangia (lah **frahn**-jah), bangs, 12

il fratello (eel frah-**tayl**-loh), brother, 29

la freccia (lah **fray**-chah), arrow, 25

freddo (**frayd**-doh), cold, 26

il freno a mano (eel **fray**-noh ah **mah**-noh), hand brake, 14

il frigorifero (eel free-goh-**ree**-fay-roh), refrigerator, 3

la frittata (lah freet-**tah**-tah), omelet, 10

la fronte (lah **frohn**-tay), forehead, 11

la frusta (la **froo**-stah), whip, 21

le frutta (lay **froot**-tah), fruit, 6

il fulmine (eel **fool**-mee-nay), lightning, 5

il fumaiolo (eel foo-migh-**oh**-loh), smokestack, 8

il fumo (eel **foo**-moh), smoke, 9

la funambola (lah foo-**nahm**-boh-lah), tightrope walker, 21

il fungo (eel **foon**-goh), mushroom, 10

il fuoco (eel foo-**oh**-koh), fire, 24

fuori (foo-**oh**-ree), outside, 26

il furgone (eel foor-**goh**-nay), van, 16

la gabbia (lah **gahb**-bee-ah), cage, 21

i gabinetti (ee **gah**-bee-nayt-tee), rest rooms, 21

la galassia (lah gah-lahs-**see**-ah), galaxy, 23

la gallina (lah gahl-**lee**-nah), hen, 9

il gallo (eel **gahl**-loh), rooster, 9

la gamba (lah **gahm**-bah), leg, 11

il garage (eel gah-**rah**-jay), garage, 14

il gattino (eel gaht-**tee**-noh), kitten, 9

il gatto (eel **gaht**-toh), cat, 9

il gatto delle nevi (eel **gaht**-toh **dayl**-lay **nay**-vee), snowmobile, 5

il gattopardo (eel gaht-toh-**pahr**-doh), leopard, 20

il gavitello (eel gah-vee-**tayl**-loh), buoy, 22

il gelato (eel jay-**lah**-toh), ice cream, 10

la gente (lah **jayn**-tay), people, 15

il gesso (eel **jays**-soh), cast, 11; chalk, 1

gettare (jayt-**tah**-ray), throw, 27

i ghiacci (ee gee-**ah**-chee), ice cubes, 3

il ghiacciaio (eel gee-ah-**chigh**-oh), glacier, 32

il ghiaccio (eel gee-**ah**-choh), ice, 5

il ghiacciolo (eel gee-ah-**choh**-loh), icicle, 5

la giacca (lah **jahk**-kah), jacket, 7

il giaguaro (eel jah-goo-**ah**-roh), jaguar, 20

giallo (**jahl**-loh), yellow, 28

il giardiniere (eel jahr-deen-ee-**ay**-ray), gardener, 15

il gigante (eel jee-**gahn**-tay), giant, 25

il gilè di piuma (eel jee-**lay** dee pee-**oo**-mah), down vest, 7

la ginnastica (lah jeen-**nah**-stee-kah), gymnastics, 18

il ginocchio (eel jee-**noh**-kee-oh), knee, 11

giocare (johk-**kah**-ray), play (a game), 27

i giocattoli (ee joh-**kaht**-toh-lee), toys, 4
il gioco (eel **joh**-koh), game, 4
il gioco degli scacchi (eel **joh**-koh **dayl**-yee **skah**-kee), chess, 4
il gioco dei birilli automatici (eel **joh**-koh **day**-ee bee-**reel**-lee ow-toh-**mah**-tee-chee), bowling, 18
il gioco della dama (eel **joh**-koh **dayl**-lah **dah**-mah), checkers, 4
il giocoliere (eel joh-koh-lee-**ay**-ray), juggler, 21
il gioielliere (eel joy-ayl-lee-**ay**-ray), jeweler, 15
il gioiello (eel joy-**ayl**-loh), jewel, 22
il giornale (eel johr-**nah**-lay), newspaper, 8
i giornali a fumetti (ee johr-**nah**-lee ah foo-**mayt**-tee), comic books, 4
il giradischi (eel jee-rah-**dee**-skee), record player, 2
la giraffa (lah jee-**rahf**-fah), giraffe, 20
il giudice (eel **joo**-dee-chay), judge, 15
la giungla (lah **joon**-glah), jungle, 32
il globo (eel **gloh**-boh), globe, 1; sphere, 30
la gobba (lah **gohb**-bah), hump, 20
la goccia di pioggia (lah **goh**-chah dee pee-**oh**-jah), raindrop, 5
il golf (eel gohlf), golf, 18; sweater, 7
il golfo (eel **gohl**-foh), gulf, 32
il gomito (eel goh-**mee**-toh), elbow, 11
la gomma (lah **gohm**-mah), eraser (pencil), 1; tire, 14
la gomma a terra (la **gohm**-mah ah **tayr**-rah), flat tire, 14
il goniometro (eel goh-nee-oh-**may**-troh), protractor, 1
la gonna (lah **gohn**-nah), skirt, 7
il gorgoglio (eel gohr-**gohl**-yoh), bubble, 22
il gorilla (eel goh-**reel**-lah), gorilla, 20
la graffa (lah **grahf**-fah), paper clip, 13
le graffette (lay grahf-**fayt**-tay), staples, 1
il granaio (el grah-**nigh**-oh), barn, 9
il granchio (eel **grahn**-chee-oh), crab, 22
grande (**grahn**-day), large, 26
il grano (eel **grah**-noh), wheat, 24
il granturco (eel grahn-**toor**-koh), corn, 24
grasso (**grahs**-soh), fat, 26
il grattacielo (eel graht-tah-**chay**-loh), skyscraper, 8
il grembiale (eel graym-bee-**ah**-lay), apron, 3
grigio (**gree**-joh), gray, 28
la griglia (lah **greel**-yah), barbecue, 5
la gru (lah groo), crane, 8
la gruccia (lah **groo**-chah), crutch, 11
la guancia (lah goo-**ahn**-chah), cheek, 11
il guanciale (eel goo-**ahn**-chah-lay), pillow, 2
i guanti (ee goo-**ahn**-tee), gloves, 7
i guanti a manopola (ee goo-**ahn**-tee ah mah-**noh**-poh-lah), mittens, 7
i guantoni (ee goo-ahn-**toh**-nee), boxing gloves, 18
guardare (goo-ahr-**dah**-ray), watch, 27
la guardia (lah goo-**ahr**-dee-ah), security guard, 13
il gufo (eel **goo**-foh), owl, 20
la guida (lah goo-**ee**-dah), tour guide, 15
guidare (goo-ee-**dah**-ray), drive, 27
il guidatore dell'autobus (eel goo-ee-dah-**toh**-ray dayl **ow**-toh-boos), bus driver, 15

l'hockey (**loh**-kay), hockey, 18

l'iceberg (ligh-**sboorg**), iceberg, 32
l'idrante (lee-**drahn**-tay), fire hydrant, 8; garden hose, 5

l'idraulico (lee-**drow**-lee-koh), plumber, 15
immaginato (eem-mah-jee-**nah**-toh), make-believe, 25
l'impermeabile (leem-payr-may-**ah**-bee-lay), raincoat, 7
l'impiegato dell'ufficio postale (leem-pee-ay-**gah**-toh day-loof-**fee**-choh poh-**stah**-lay), postal worker, 13
in giù (een joo), down, 26
in su (een soo), up, 26
l'incrocio (lee-**kroh**-choh), intersection, 16
l'incudine (leen-**koo**-dee-nay), anvil, 25
indietro (een-dee-**ay**-troh), inside, 26
l'indirizzo (leen-dee-**ree**-tsoh), address, 13
l'indirizzo del mittente (leen-dee-**ree**-tsoh dayl mee-**tayn**-tay), return address, 13
l'indossatrice (leen-dohs-sah-**tree**-chay), model, 15
infelice (een-fay-**lee**-chay), sad, 26
l'infermiere (leen-fayr-mee-**ay**-ray), nurse, 11
innaffiare (een-nahf-fee-**ah**-ray), water, 27
l'insalata (leen-sah-**lah**-tah), salad, 10
insegnare (een-say-**nyah**-ray), teach, 27
l'insetto (leen-**sayt**-toh), insect, 24
l'intasamento (leen-ta-zah-**mayn**-toh), traffic jam, 8
l'inverno (leen-**vayr**-noh), winter, 5
l'ippopotamo (leep-poh-**poh**-tah-moh), hippopotamus, 20
l'isola (**lee**-zoh-lah), island, 32
l'istituto di bellezza (lee-stee-**too**-toh dee bayl-**lay**-tsah), beauty salon, 12

i jeans (ee jeens), jeans, 7
il jeep (eel jeep), jeep, 16

il ketchup (eel ketchup), ketchup, 10

le labbra (lay **lahb**-brah), lips, 11
il laboratorio (eel lah-boh-rah-**toh**-ree-oh), laboratory, 23
il lago (eel **lah**-goh), lake, 32
la lampada (lah **lahm**-pah-dah), lamp, 2
la lampadina (lah lahm-pah-**dee**-nah), lightbulb, 4, 21
la lampadina tascabile (lah lahm-pah-**dee**-nah tah-**skah**-bee-lay), flashlight, 3
i lamponi (ee lahm-**poh**-nee), raspberries, 6
la lancetta (lah lahn-**chayt**-tah), hand, 1
la lancia (lah **lahn**-chah), lance, 25; spear, 24
largo (**lahr**-goh), wide, 26
il latte (eel **laht**-tay), milk, 6
la lattuga (lah laht-**too**-gah), lettuce, 6
la lavagna (lah lah-**vah**-nyah), chalkboard, 1
la lavanderia (lah lah-vahn-day-**ree**-ah), utility room, 3
il lavapiatti (eel lah-vah-pee-**aht**-tee), dishwasher, 3
lavarsi (lah-**vahr**-see), wash (oneself), 27
la lavatrice (lah lah-vah-**tree**-chay), washing machine, 3
leggere (**layj**-jay-ray), read, 27
leggero (layj-**jay**-roh), light, 26
il legno (eel **lay**-nyoh), wood, 3
le lentiggini (lay layn-**teej**-jee-nee), freckles, 12
lento (**layn**-toh), slow, 26
la lenza (lah **layn**-zah), fishing line, 22
il lenzuolo (eel layn-zoo-**oh**-loh), sheet, 2
il leone (eel lay-**oh**-nay), lion, 20, 21
la lettera (lah **layt**-tay-rah), letter, 13

il letto (eel **layt**-toh), bed, 2
la libreria (lah lee-bray-**ree**-ah), bookstore, 8
il libretto d'assegni (eel lee-**brayt**-toh dahs-**say**-nyee), checkbook, 13
il libro (eel **lee**-broh), book, 1
il libro di disegni (eel **lee**-broh dee dee-**zay**-nyee), coloring book, 4
la lima (lah **lee**-mah), file, 3
la limaiola (lah lee-migh-**oh**-lah), nail file, 12
il limone (eel lee-**moh**-nay), lemon, 6
la lingua (lah **leen**-goo-ah), tongue, 11
lisci (**lee**-shee), straight, 12
lontano (lohn-**tah**-noh), far, 26
la lotta sportiva (lah **loht**-tah spohr-**tee**-vah), wrestling, 18
la lucertola (lah loo-**chayr**-toh-lah), lizard, 20
le luci dei freni (lay **loo**-chee **day**-ee **fray**-nee), brake lights, 14
la luna (lah **loo**-nah), moon, 23
lunghi (**loon**-gee), long, 12
lungo (**loon**-goh), long, 26
il lupo (eel **loo**-poh), wolf, 20
il lupo di mare (eel **loo**-poh dee **mah**-ray), barnacle, 22

le macchie (lay **mahk**-kee-ay), spots, 20
la macchina (lah **mahk**-kee-nah), car, 16
la macchina da corsa (lah **mahk**-kee-nah dah **kohr**-sah), race car, 14
la macchina da polizia (lah **mahk**-kee-nah dah poh-lee-**tsee**-ah), police car, 16
la macchina da scrivere (lah **mahk**-kee-nah dah skree-**vay**-ray), typewriter, 13
la macchina fotografica (lah **mahk**-kee-nah foh-toh-**grah**-fee-kah), camera, 17, 21
la macchina lunare (lah **mahk**-kee-nah loo-**nah**-ray), lunar rover, 23
la macchina per cucire (lah **mahk**-kee-nah payr koo-**chee**-ray), sewing machine, 19
il macellaio (eel mah-chay-**ligh**-oh), butcher, 15
la macelleria (lah mah-chayl-lay-**ree**-ah), butcher shop, 8
la madre (lah **mah**-dray), mother, 29
la maestra (lah mah-**ay**-strah), teacher (female), 1
il maestro (eel mah-**ay**-stroh), teacher (male), 1
la maga (lah **mah**-gah), fairy, 25
la maglia di ferro (lah **mahl**-yah dee **fayr**-roh), chain mail, 25
la maglietta (lah mahl-**yayt**-tah), T-shirt, 7
la maglietta sportiva (lah mahl-**yayt**-tah spohr-**tee**-vah), sweatshirt, 7
il magnete (eel mah-**nyay**-tay), magnet, 4
il magnetofono (eel mah-nyay-**toh**-foh-noh), cassette player, 2
il mago (eel **mah**-goh), magician, 21
magro (**mah**-groh), thin, 26
il maiale (eel migh-**ah**-lay), pig, 9
male (**mah**-lay), bad, 26
la mamma (lah **mahm**-mah), mom, 29
il mammùt (eel mahm-**moot**), mammoth, 24
mangiare (mahn-**jah**-ray), eat, 27
la manica (lah **mah**-nee-kah), sleeve, 7
il manicotto dell'aria (eel mah-nee-**koht**-toh dayl-**lah**-ree-ah), air hose, 14
la manicure (lah mah-nee-**koo**-ray), manicurist, 12
la maniglia (lah mah-**neel**-yah), door handle, 14
la mano (lah **mah**-noh), hand, 11
il manovale (eel mah-noh-**vah**-lay), construction worker, 15
la mantellina (lah mahn-tayl-**lee**-nah), cape, 21

il manubrio di bicicletta (eel mah-**noo**-bree-oh dee bee-chee-klayt-tah), handlebars, 14

il marciapiede (eel mahr-chah-pee-**ay**-day), sidewalk, 16

il mare (eel **mah**-ray), sea, 32

il marinaio (eel mah-ree-**nigh**-oh), sailor, 15

la marmellata (lah mahr-mayl-**lah**-tah), jam, 10

marrone (mahr-**roh**-nay), brown, 28

il martello (eel mahr-**tayl**-loh), hammer, 3

la mascara (lah **mah**-skah-rah), mascara, 12

la maschera (lah **mah**-skay-rah), mask, 19, 22

il masso (eel **mahs**-soh), boulder, 24

la matita (lah **mah**-tee-tah), pencil, 1

le matite colorate (lay mah-**tee**-tay koh-loh-**rah**-tay), colored pencils, 1

il mattone (eel maht-**toh**-nay), brick, 3

la mazza (lah **mah**-tsah), bat, 18

la mazza da golf (lah **mah**-tsah dah gohlf), golf club, 18

il meccanico (eel mayk-**kah**-nee-koh), mechanic, 14

la medaglia (lah may-**dahl**-yah), medal, 18

la medicina (lah may-dee-**chee**-nah), medicine, 11

dal medico (dahl **may**-dee-koh), doctor's office, 11

medio (**may**-dee-oh), medium, 26

la medusa (lah may-**doo**-sah), jellyfish, 22

la mela (lah **may**-lah), apple, 6

la mela caramellata (lah **may**-lah kah-rah-mayl-**lah**-tah), caramel apple, 21

il melone (eel may-**loh**-nay), melon, 6

il menestrello (eel may-nay-**strayl**-loh), minstrel, 25

il mento (eel **mayn**-toh), chin, 11

il menù (eel may-**noo**), menu, 10

la merce imbarcata (lah **mayr**-chay eem-bahr-**kah**-tah), cargo bay, 23

metà (may-**tah**), half, 31

il meteorologo (eel may-tay-oh-**roh**-loh-goh), weather forecaster, 15

il metro a nastro (eel **may**-troh ah **nah**-stroh), tape measure, 3

il microfono (eel mee-**kroh**-foh-noh), microphone, 19

il microscopio (eel mee-kroh-**skoh**-pee-oh), microscope, 23

miliardo (meel-**yahr**-doh), billion, 31

milione (meel-**yoh**-nay), million, 31

mille (**meel**-lay), one thousand, 31

il miscelatore (eel mee-shay-lah-**toh**-ray), electric mixer, 3

il missile (eel **mees**-see-lay), rocket, 23

il molo (eel **moh**-loh), dock, 16

la moneta (lah moh-**nay**-tah), coin, 13

il monopattino (eel moh-noh-paht-**tee**-noh), scooter, 16

la montagna (lah mohn-**tah**-nyah), mountains, 32

morbido (**mohr**-bee-doh), soft, 26

la mosca (lah **moh**-skah), fly, 5

la mostarda (lah moh-**stahr**-dah), mustard, 10

la mostra dei talenti (lah **moh**-strah **day**-ee tah-**layn**-tee), talent show, 19

mostrare (moh-**strah**-ray), point (at), 27

la motocicletta (lah moh-toh-chee-**klayt**-tah), motorcycle, 16

il motore (eel moh-**toh**-ray), engine, 14, 17

il motoscafo (eel moh-toh-**skah**-foh), motorboat, 16

il mousse (eel moos), mousse, 12

la mucca (lah **mook**-kah), cow, 9

il museo (eel moo-**zay**-oh), museum, 8

la muta (lah **moo**-tah), wet suit, 22

il naso (eel **nah**-zo), nose, 11

il nastro d'imballaggio (eel **nah**-stroh deem-bahl-**lahj**-joh), packing tape, 13

la nave (lah **nah**-vay), cruise ship, 16

la navicella spaziale (lah nah-vee-**chayl**-lah spah-tsee-**ah**-lay), space shuttle, 23

il navigatore (eel nah-vee-gah-**toh**-ray), navigator, 17

la nebbia (lah **nayb**-bee-ah), fog, 5

la nebulosa (lah nay-boo-**loh**-zah), nebula, 23

il negozio dei gioccattoli (eel nay-**goh**-tsee-oh day-ee joh-**kaht**-toh-lee), toy store, 8

il negozio di confezioni (eel nay-**goh**-tsee-oh dee kohn-fay-tsee- **oh**-nee), clothing store, 8

neri (**nay**-ree), black, 12

nero (**nay**-roh), black, 28

la neve (lah **nay**-vay), snow, 5

il nido (eel **nee**-doh), bird's nest, 5

le noci (lay **noh**-chee), nuts, 6

il nodo (eel **noh**-doh), knot, 13

non tagliente (nohn tahl-**yayn**-tay), dull, 26

la nonna (lah **nohn**-nah), grandma, grandmother, 29

il nonno (eel **nohn**-noh), grandfather, grandpa, 29

nono (**noh**-noh), ninth, 31

nord (nohrd), north, 32

nord-est (nohrd-**ayst**), northeast, 32

nord-ovest (nohrd-oh-**vayst**), northwest, 32

la notte (lah **noht**-tay), night, 21

novanta (noh-**vahn**-tah), ninety, 31

novantacinque (noh-vahn-tah-**cheen**-kway), ninety-five, 31

novantadue (noh-vahn-tah-**doo**-ay), ninety-two, 31

novantanove (noh-vahn-tah-**noh**-vay), ninety-nine, 31

novantaquattro (noh-vahn-tah-**kwaht**-troh), ninety-four, 31

novantasei (noh-vahn-tah-**say**-ee), ninety-six, 31

novantasette (noh-vahn-tah-**sayt**-tay), ninety-seven, 31

novantatrè (noh-vahn-tah-**tray**), ninety-three, 31

novantotto (noh-vahn-**toht**-toh), ninety-eight, 31

novantuno (noh-vahn-**too**-noh), ninety-one, 31

nove (**noh**-vay), nine, 31

i numeri (ee **noo**-may-ree), numbers, 1, 31

i numeri cardinali (ee **noo**-may-ree kahr-dee-**nah**-lee), cardinal numbers, 31

i numeri ordinali (ee **noo**-may-ree ohr-dee-**nah**-lee), ordinal numbers, 31

nuotare (noo-oh-**tah**-ray), swim, 27

il nuoto (eel noo-**oh**-toh), swimming, 18

nuovo (noo-**oh**-voh), new, 26

le nuvole (lay **noo**-voh-lay), clouds, 5

l'oasi (**loh**-ah-zee), oasis, 32

l'oblò (loh-**bloh**), porthole, 22

l'oca (**loh**-kah), goose, 9

gli occhi (lyee **oh**-kee), eyes, 11

gli occhiali (lyee oh-kee-**ah**-lee), glasses, 7

gli occhiali di protezione (lyee oh-kee-**ah**-lee dee proh-tay-tsee- **oh**-nay), goggles, 18

gli occhiali scuri (lyee oh-kee-**ah**-lee **skoo**-ree), sunglasses, 7

l'oceano (loh-chay-**ah**-noh), ocean, 22

l'Oceano Artico (loh-chay-**ah**-noh **ahr**-tee-koh), Arctic Ocean, 32

l'Oceano Atlantico (loh-chay-**ah**-noh aht-**lahn**-tee-koh), Atlantic Ocean, 32

l'Oceano Indiano (loh-chay-**ah**-noh een-dee-**ah**-noh), Indian Ocean, 32

l'Oceano Pacifico (loh-chay-**ah**-noh pah-**chee**-fee-koh), Pacific Ocean, 32

l'olio (**loh**-lee-oh), oil, 14

l'ombra (**lohm**-brah), shadow, 9

l'ombrello (lohm-**brayl**-loh), umbrella, 4, 7

l'onda (**lohn**-dah), wave, 22

ondulati (ohn-doo-**lah**-tee), wavy, 12

l'operaia (loh-pay-**righ**-ah), factory worker, 15

l'orchestra (lohr-**kay**-strah), orchestra, 19

l'orecchino (loh-ray-**kee**-noh), earring, 7

l'orecchio (loh-**ray**-kee-oh), ear, 11

l'orma (**lohr**-mah), footprint, 23

l'oro (**loh**-roh), gold, 22

l'orologio (loh-roh-**loh**-joh), clock, 1; watch, 7

l'orsacchiotto (lohr-sah-kee-**oht**-toh), bear cub, 20; teddy bear, 4

l'orso (**lohr**-soh), bear, 20

l'orso bianco (**lohr**-soh bee-**ahn**-koh), polar bear, 20

l'orso panda (**lohr**-soh **pahn**-dah), panda, 20

gli ortaggi (lyee ohr-**tahj**-jee), vegetables, 6

l'orto (**lohr**-toh), vegetable garden, 5

l'ospedale (loh-spay-**dah**-lay), hospital, 8

l'osso (**lohs**-soh), bone, 24

l'ostrica (**loh**-stree-kah), clam, 22

l'ottagono (loht-**tah**-goh-noh), octagon, 30

ottanta (oht-**tahn**-tah), eighty, 31

ottantacinque (oht-tahn-tah-**cheen**-kway), eighty-five, 31

ottantadue (oht-tahn-tah-**doo**-ay), eighty-two, 31

ottantanove (oht-tahn-tah-**noh**-vay), eighty-nine, 31

ottantaquattro (oht-tahn-tah-**kwaht**-troh), eighty-four, 31

ottantasei (oht-tahn-tah-**say**-ee), eighty-six, 31

ottantasette (oht-tahn-tah-**sayt**-tay), eighty-seven, 31

ottantatrè (oht-tahn-tah-**tray**), eighty-three, 31

ottantotto (oht-tahn-**toht**-toh), eighty-eight, 31

ottantuno (oht-tahn-**too**-noh), eighty-one, 31

ottavo (oht-**tah**-voh), eighth, 31

l'ottico (**loht**-tee-koh), optician, 15

otto (**oht**-toh), eight, 31

l'ovale (loh-**vah**-lay), oval, 30

ovest (oh-**vayst**), west, 32

il pacco (eel **pahk**-koh), package, 13

il pacco per la spesa (eel **pahk**-koh payr lah **spay**-zah), shopping bag, 6

la padella (lah pah-**dayl**-lah), pan, 3

il padre (eel **pah**-dray), father, 29

il paese (eel pah-**ay**-say), country, 9

il pagliaccio (eel pahl-**yah**-choh), clown, 21

la pala (lah **pah**-lah), shovel, 5

il palcoscenico (eel pahl-koh-**shay**-nee-koh), stage, 19

la paletta della spazzatura (lah pah-**layt**-tah **dayl**-lah spah-tsah-**too**-rah), dustpan, 3

la palla (lah **pahl**-lah), baseball, football, soccer ball, 18

la pallacanestro (lah pahl-lah-kah-**nay**-stroh), basketball, 18

la pallavolo (lah pahl-**lah**-voh-loh), volleyball, 18

le palline di marmo (lay pahl-**lee**-nay dee **mahr**-moh), marbles, 4

il pallone (eel pahl-**loh**-nay), balloon, 21; hot-air balloon, 16

la palotta di neve (lah pah-**loht**-tah dee **nay**-vay), snowball, 5

la panca (lah **pahn**-kah), bench, 8

il pane (eel **pah**-nay), bread, 6

la panetteria (lah pahn-ayt-tay-**ree**-ah), bakery, 8

la panna (lah **pahn**-nah), cream, 10
il **pannello di controllo** (eel pahn-**nayl**-loh dee kohn-**trohl**-loh), control panel, 23
il **pannello solare** (eel pahn-**nayl**-loh soh-**lah**-ray), solar panel, 23
il **panno** (eel **pahn**-noh), cloth, 24
i **pantaloni** (ee pahn-tah-**loh**-nee), pants, 7
i **pantaloni della tuta** (ee pahn-tah-**loh**-nee **dayl**-lah **too**-tah), sweatpants, 7
il **papero** (eel **pah**-pay-roh), gosling, 9
il **pappagallo** (eel pahp-pah-**gahl**-loh), parrot, 20
il **parabrezza** (eel pah-rah-**bray**-tsah), windshield, 14
il **paracadute** (eel pah-rah-kah-**doo**-tay), parachute, 18
il **paracadutismo** (eel pah-rah-kah-doo-**teez**-moh), skydiving, 18
il **paraorecchie** (eel pah-rah-oh-**ray**-kee-ay), earmuffs, 7
la **parata di circo** (lah pah-**rah**-tah dee **cheer**-koh), circus parade, 21
il **paraurti** (eel pahr-ah-**oor**-tee), fender, 14
il **parcheggio** (eel pahr-**kay**-joh), parking lot, 8
il **parchimetro** (eel pahr-kee-**may**-troh), parking meter, 8
il **parco** (eel **pahr**-koh), park, 8
il **parco giochi** (eel **pahr**-koh joh-kee), playground, 8
la **parete** (lah pah-**ray**-tay), wall, 2
parlare (pahr-**lah**-ray), talk, 27
la **parrucca** (lah pahr-**rook**-kah), wig, 19
la **parrucchiera** (lah pahr-roo-kee-**ay**-rah), hairstylist, 12
il **passaggio pedonale** (eel pahs-**sah**-joh pay-doh-**nah**-lay), crosswalk, 16
il **passaporto** (eel pahs-sah-**pohr**-toh), passport, 17
il **passeggero** (eel pahs-say-**jay**-roh), passenger, 17
il **passeggino** (eel pahs-say-**jee**-noh), stroller, 16
il **passeggio nello spazio** (eel pahs-**say**-joh **nayl**-loh spah-tsee-oh), space walk, 23
la **pasta** (lah **pah**-stah), noodles, 10
il **pastello** (eel pah-**stayl**-loh), crayon, 1
i **pasti** (ee **pah**-stee), meals, 10
le **patate** (lay pah-**tah**-tay), potatoes, 6
le **patatine** (lay pah-tah-**tee**-nay), potato chips
le **patatine fritte** (lay pah-tah-**tee**-nay **freet**-tay), french fries, 10
il **pattinaggio** (eel paht-tee-**nah**-joh), skating, 18
pattinare (paht-tee-**nah**-ray), skate, 27
i **pattini** (ee paht-**tee**-nee), skates, 18
i **pattini a rotelle** (ee paht-**tee**-nee ah roh-**tayl**-lay), roller skates, 16
il **pavimento** (eel pah-vee-**mayn**-toh), floor, 2
il **pavone** (eel pah-**voh**-nay), peacock, 20
il **paziente** (eel pah-tsee-**ayn**-tay), patient, 11
la **pecora** (lah **pay**-koh-rah), sheep, 9
il **pedale** (eel pay-**dah**-lay), pedal, 14
la **pedicure** (lah pay-dee-**koo**-ray), pedicurist, 12
la **pelliccia** (lah payl-**lee**-chah), fur, 24
la **pellicola** (lah payl-**lee**-koh-lah), film, 21
la **penisola** (lah pay-**nee**-zoh-lah), peninsula, 32
la **penna** (lah **payn**-nah), pen, 1
il **pennello** (eel payn-**nayl**-loh), paintbrush, 1
pensare (payn-**sah**-ray), think, 27
il **pepe** (eel **pay**-pay), pepper, 10
la **perforatrice per carta** (lah payr-foh-rah-**tree**-chay payr **kahr**-tah), hole punch, 1
le **persiane** (lay payr-zee-**ah**-nay), venetian blinds, 2
pesante (pay-**zahn**-tay), heavy, 26

la **pesca** (lah **pay**-skah), (sport) fishing, 24
la **pesca** (lah **pay**-skah), (fruit) peach, 6
il **pescatore** (eel pay-skah-**toh**-ray), fisherman, 15
il **pesce** (eel **pay**-shay), fish, 1, 10
il **pesce angelo** (eel **pay**-shay ahn-**jay**-loh), angelfish, 22
il **pesce spada** (eel **pay**-shay **spah**-dah), swordfish, 22
il **petalo** (eel **pay**-tah-loh), petal, 5
il **pettine** (eel **payt**-tee-nay), comb, 12
il **petto** (eel **payt**-toh), chest, 11
il **pianeta** (eel pee-ah-**nay**-tah), planet, 23
piangere (pee-**ahn**-jay-ray), cry, 27
il **pianoforte** (eel pee-ah-noh-**fohr**-tay), piano, 19
la **pianta** (lah pee-**ahn**-tah), plant, 1
la **pianura** (lah pee-ah-**noo**-rah), plain, 32
i **piatti** (ee pee-**ah**-tee), cymbals, 19; dishes, 3
il **piattino** (eel pee-aht-**tee**-noh), saucer, 10
il **piatto** (eel pee-**aht**-toh), plate, 10
la **piazza** (lah pee-**ah**-tsah), square, 8
il **piccino** (eel pee-**chee**-noh), baby, 9
i **piccoli soldati** (ee **peek**-koh-lee sohl-**dah**-tee), toy soldiers, 4
piccolo (**peek**-koh-loh), small, 26
il **picnic** (eel **peek**-neek), picnic, 9
il **piede** (eel pee-**ay**-day), foot, 11
pieno (pee-**ay**-noh), full, 26
la **pigiama** (lah pee-**jah**-mah), pajamas, 7
la **pillola** (lah **peel**-loh-lah), pill, 11
il **pilota** (eel pee-**loh**-tah), pilot, 17
il **ping-pong** (eel **peeng**-pohng), table tennis, 18
il **pinguino** (eel peen-goo-**ee**-noh), penguin, 20
la **pinna** (lah **peen**-nah), fin, 22; flipper, 22
la **pinza** (lah **peen**-tsah), pliers, 14
la **pioggia** (lah pee-**ohj**-jah), rain, 5
la **pioggia dei meteori** (lah pee-**ohj**-jah **day**-ee may-**tay**-oh-ree), meteor shower, 23
il **pipistrello** (eel pee-pee-**strayl**-loh), bat, 25
la **piscina** (lah pee-**shee**-nah), swimming pool, 18
i **piselli** (ee pee-**sayl**-lee), peas, 6
la **pista** (lah **pee**-stah), runway, 17
il **pittore** (eel peet-**toh**-ray), painter, 15
la **piuma** (lah pee-**oo**-mah), feather, 4
le **piume** (lay pee-**oo**-may), feathers, 20
il **poliziotto** (eel poh-lee-tsee-**oht**-toh), policeman, 15
il **pollice** (eel **pohl**-lee-chay), thumb, 11
il **pollo** (eel **pohl**-loh), chicken, 10
il **polo Nord** (eel **poh**-loh nohrd), North Pole, 32
il **polo Sud** (eel **poh**-loh sood), South Pole, 32
il **polpo** (eel **pohl**-poh), octopus, 22
la **poltrona** (lah pohl-**troh**-nah), armchair, 2
il **polvere** (eel **pohl**-vay-ray), dust, 4
i **pomodori** (ee poh-moh-**doh**-ree), tomatoes, 6
la **pompa della benzina** (lah **pohm**-pah **dayl**-lah bayn-**tsee**-nah), gas pump, 14
il **pompelmo** (eel pohm-**payl**-moh), grapefruit, 6
il **pompiere** (eel pohm-pee-**ay**-ray), fire fighter, 15
il **ponte** (eel **pohn**-tay), bridge, 16
il **ponte levatoio** (eel **pohn**-tay lay-vah-**toy**-oh), drawbridge, 25
il **popcorn** (eel **pohp**-kohrn), popcorn, 21
il **porcellino** (eel pohr-chayl-**lee**-noh), piglet, 9
la **porta** (lah **pohr**-tah), door, 2; gate, 17
il **portabagagli** (eel pohr-tah-bah-**gahl**-yee), trunk, 14
il **portabaglio** (eel pohr-tah-bah-**gahl**-yo), baggage handler, 17
il **portafoglio** (eel pohr-tah-**fohl**-yoh), wallet, 13
portare (pohr-**tah**-ray), carry, 27
il **portiere** (eel pohr-tee-**ay**-ray), doorman, 15
il **posapiedi** (eel poh-zah-pee-**ay**-dee), footstool, 2

il **postino** (eel poh-**stee**-noh), letter carrier, 15
il **posto di polizia** (eel **poh**-stoh dee poh-lee-**tsee**-ah), police station, 8
la **pozzanghera** (lah poh-**tsahn**-gay-rah), puddle, 5
il **pozzo** (eel **poh**-tsoh), well, 24
il **pranzo** (eel **prahn**-tsoh), lunch, 10
il **pranzo surgelato** (eel **prahn**-tsoh soor-jay-**lah**-toh), frozen dinner, 6
prendere (**prayn**-day-ray), catch, 27
i **preposizioni** (ee pray-poh-zee-tsee-**oh**-nee), prepositions, 26
la **presa** (lah **pray**-tsah), electrical outlet, 3
il **presentatore** (eel pray-zayn-tah-**toh**-ray), ringmaster, 21
il **prezzo** (eel **pray**-tsoh), price, 6
la **primavera** (lah pree-mah-**vay**-rah), spring, 5
primo (**pree**-moh), first, 31
il **principe** (eel **preen**-chee-pay), prince, 25
la **principessa** (la preen-chee-**pays**-sah), princess, 25
il **problema d'aritmetica** (eel proh-**blay**-mah dah-reet-**may**-tee-kah), arithmetic problem, 1
la **proboscide** (lah proh-boh-**shee**-day), trunk, 24
il **programmatore** (eel proh-grahm-mah-**toh**-ray), computer programmer, 15
il **proiettore** (eel proy-ayt-**toh**-ray), movie projector, 4
il **prontosoccorso** (eel **prohn**-toh sohk-**kohr**-soh), ambulance, 16
il **prosciutto** (eel proh-**shoot**-toh), ham, 10
la **provetta** (lah proh-**vayt**-tah), test tube, 23
il **pterodattilo** (eel tay-roh-**daht**-tee-loh), pterodactyl, 24
il **pubblico** (eel **poob**-blee-koh), audience, 19
il **pugilato** (eel poo-jee-**lah**-toh), boxing, 18
il **pulcino** (eel pool-**chee**-noh), chick, 9
il **puledro** (eel poo-**lay**-droh), colt, 9
pulito (poo-**lee**-toh), clean, 26
la **punta di freccia** (lah **poon**-tah dee **fray**-chah), arrowhead, 24

il **quaderno** (eel kwah-**dayr**-noh), notebook, 1
il **quadrato** (eel kwah-**drah**-toh), square, 30
il **quadro** (eel **kwah**-droh), picture, 1
quaranta (kwah-**rahn**-tah), forty, 31
quarantacinque (kwah-rahn-tah-**cheen**-kway), forty-five, 31
quarantadue (kwah-rahn-tah-**doo**-ay), forty-two, 31
quarantanove (kwah-rahn-tah-**noh**-vay), forty-nine, 31
quarantaquattro (kwah-rahn-tah-**kwaht**-troh), forty-four, 31
quarantasei (kwah-rahn-tah-**say**-ee), forty-six, 31
quarantasette (kwah-rahn-tah-**sayt**-tay), forty-seven, 31
quarantatrè (kwah-rahn-tah-**tray**), forty-three, 31
quarantotto (kwah-rahn-**toht**-toh), forty-eight, 31
quarantuno (kwah-rahn-**too**-noh), forty-one, 31
quarto (**kwahr**-toh), fourth, 31
quattordici (kwaht-**tohr**-dee-chee), fourteen, 31
quattro (**kwaht**-troh), four, 5, 31
quindici (**kween**-dee-chee), fifteen, 31
quinto (**kween**-toh), fifth, 31

la **racchetta** (lah rahk-**kayt**-tah), racket, 18; tennis racket, 17
la **raccolta** (lah rahk-**kohl**-tah), crop, 24

la radio (lah **rah**-dee-oh), radio, 2
la ragazza (lah rah-**gah**-tsah), girl, 9
i ragazzi (ee rah-**gah**-tsee), children, 19
il ragazzo (eel rah-**gah**-tsoh), boy, 9
i raggi (ee **rahj**-jee), spokes, 14
i raggi X (ee **rahj**-jee eeks), X ray, 11
la ragnatela (lah rah-nyah-**tay**-lah), cobweb, 4;
   spiderweb, 25
il ragno (eel **rah**-nyoh), spider, 25
il ramo (eel **rah**-moh), branch, 5
la rana (lah **rah**-nah), frog, 9
rapido (**rah**-pee-doh), fast, 26
il rasoio (eel rah-**zoy**-oh), razor, 12
il rastrello (eel rah-**strayl**-loh), rake, 5
il ratto (eel **raht**-toh), rat, 25
la razza (lah **rah**-tsah), stingray, 22
il re (eel ray), king, 25
il recinto (eel ray-**cheen**-toh), fence, 9
il recinto con sabbia (eel ray-**cheen**-toh kohn
   sahb-bee-ah), sandbox, 8
il regalo (eel ray-**gah**-loh), gift, 10
la regina (lah ray-**jee**-nah), queen, 25
la regola (lah **ray**-goh-lah), ruler, 1
il relitto di nave naufragio (eel ray-**leet**-toh dee
   nah-vay now-**frah**-joh), shipwreck, 22
il remo (eel **ray**-moh), oar, 16
la rete (lah **ray**-tay), net, 18
la rete di sicurezza (lah **ray**-tay dee
   see-koo-**ray**-tsah), safety net, 21
il rettangolo (eel rayt-**tahn**-goh-loh), rectangle, 30
il revelatore del metallo (eel ray-vay-lah-**toh**-ray
   dayl may-**tahl**-loh), metal detector, 17
ricci (**ree**-chee), curly, 12
il riccio di mare (eel **ree**-choh dee **mah**-ray), sea
   urchin, 22
ricevere (ree-**chay**-vay-ray), receive, 27
ridere (**ree**-day-ray), laugh, 27
il riflettore (eel ree-flay-**toh**-ray), flashbulb, 21
i riflettori (ee ree-flayt-**toh**-ree), reflectors, 14
il rimorchiatore (eel ree-mohr-kee-ah-**toh**-ray),
   tugboat, 16
il rinoceronte (eel ree-noh-chay-**rohn**-tay),
   rhinoceros, 20
il riso (eel **ree**-zoh), rice, 10
il ristorante (eel ree-stoh-**rahn**-tay), restaurant,
   8, 10
il ritiro bagagli (eel ree-**tee**-roh bah-**gahl**-yee),
   baggage claim, 17
le riviste (lay ree-**vee**-stay), magazines, 11
il robot (eel **roh**-boht), robot, 23
la roccia (lah **roh**-chah), rock, 24
rompere (**rohm**-pay-ray), break, 27
il rompicapo (eel rohm-pee-**kah**-poh), jigsaw
   puzzle, 4
rosa (**roh**-zah), pink, 28
il rossetto (eel rohs-**sayt**-toh), lipstick, 12
rossi (**rohs**-see), red, 12
rosso (**rohs**-soh), red, 28
il rosso d'uovo (eel **rohs**-soh doo-**oh**-voh), yolk,
   10
le rotaie (lay roh-**tigh**-ay), train tracks, 9
il rubinetto (eel roo-bee-**nayt**-toh), faucet, 3
ruggire (roo-**jee**-ray), roar, 27
la ruota (lah roo-**oh**-tah), wheel, 24
la ruota di carretta (lah roo-**oh**-tah dee
   kahr-**rayt**-tah), cartwheel, 21
le ruote speciali (lay roo-**oh**-tay spay-**chah**-lee),
   training wheels, 14

la sabbia (lah **sahb**-bee-ah), sand, 22
il sacco a pelo (eel **sahk**-koh ah **pay**-loh),
   sleeping bag, 9

il sacco da posta (eel **sahk**-koh da **poh**-stah),
   mailbag, 13
il sacco per abiti (eel **sahk**-koh payr **ah**-bee-tee),
   garment bag, 17
la sala da pranzo (lah **sah**-lah dah **prahn**-zoh),
   dining room, 2
il sale (eel **sah**-lay), salt, 10
salire (sah-**lee**-ray), climb, 27
il salotto (eel sah-**loht**-toh), living room, 2
le salsicce (lay sahl-**see**-chay), sausages, 10
saltare (sahl-**tah**-ray), jump, 27
il salto in alto (eel **sahl**-toh een **ahl**-toh), high
   jump, 18
il salto in lungo (eel **sahl**-toh een **loon**-goh), long
   jump, 18
il salto mortale (eel **sahl**-toh mohr-**tah**-lay),
   somersault, 21
il salvadanaio (eel sahl-vah-dah-**nigh**-oh), piggy
   bank, 13
i sandali (ee **sahn**-dah-lee), sandals, 7
il sangue (eel **sahn**-gway), blood, 11
il sapone (eel sah-**poh**-nay), soap, 6
il saracco (eel sah-**rahk**-koh), saw, 3
il sarto (eel **sahr**-toh), tailor, 15
il sassofono (eel sahs-**soh**-foh-noh), saxophone,
   19
il satellite (eel sah-tayl-**lee**-tay), satellite, 23
lo scaffale (loh skahf-**fah**-lay), bookcase, 1;
   shelf, 2
le scaglie (lay **skahl**-yay), scales, 22
la scala a pioli (lah **skah**-lah ah pee-**oh**-lee),
   ladder, 23
la scala di sicurezza (lah **skah**-lah dee
   see-koo-**ray**-tsah), fire escape, 8
la scala mobile (lah **skah**-lah **moh**-bee-lay),
   escalator, 17
la scala per arrampicarsi (lah **skah**-lah payr
   ahr-rahm-pee-**kahr**-see), rope ladder, 21
le scale (lay **skah**-lay), stairs, 2
le scarpe (lay **skahr**-pay), shoes, 7
le scarpe da tennis (lay skahr-**pay** dah
   tayn-nees), gym shoes, 7
le scarpette da ballo (lay skahr-**payt**-tay dah
   bahl-loh), ballet slippers, 19
gli scarponi (lyee skahr-**poh**-nee), hiking boots, 7
la scatola (lah **skah**-toh-lah), box, 4; can, 6
la scatola degli utensili (lah **skah**-toh-lah
   dayl-yee oo-**tayn**-zee-lee), toolbox, 3
la scatola della musica (lah **skah**-toh-lah
   dayl-lah **moo**-zee-kah), music box, 4
scavare (skah-**vah**-ray), dig, 27
il scenario (eel shay-**nahr**-ee-oh), scenery, 19
lo schedario (loh skay-**dah**-ree-oh), file cabinet,
   13
lo scheletro (loh skay-**lay**-troh), skeleton, 24
lo schermo di radar (loh **skayr**-moh dee
   rah-dahr), radar screen, 17
la schiena (lah skee-**ay**-nah), back, 11
la schiuma di sapone (lah **skyoo**-mah dee
   sah-**poh**-nay), suds, 6
gli sci (lyee shee), skis, 18
lo sci alpino (loh shee ahl-**pee**-noh), downhill
   skiing, 18
sciare (shah-**ray**), ski, 27
la sciarpa (lah **shahr**-pah), scarf, 7
lo scienziato (loh shayn-zee-**ah**-toh), scientist,
   23
la scimmia (lah **sheem**-mee-ah), monkey, 20
la scivola (lah **shee**-voh-lah), slide, 8
la scodella (lah skoh-**dayl**-lah), bowl, 10
la scopa (lah **skoh**-pah), broom, 3
la scopa di stracci (lah **skoh**-pah dee
   strah-chee), mop, 3

la scriminatura (lah skree-mee-nah-**too**-rah),
   part, 12
scrivere (**skree**-vay-ray), write, 27
lo scudiero (loh skoo-dee-**ay**-roh), squire, 25
lo scudo (loh **skoo**-doh), shield, 25
la scuola (lah skoo-**oh**-lah), school, 8
scuro (**skoo**-roh), dark, 26
la secchia (lah **say**-kee-ah), bucket, 24
secco (**say**-koh), dry, 26
la seconda pilota (lah say-**kohn**-dah
   pee-**loh**-tah), copilot, 17
secondo (say-**kohn**-doh), second, 31
il sedano (eel **say**-dah-noh), celery, 10
sedersi (say-**dayr**-see), sit down, 27
la sedia (lah **say**-dee-ah), chair, 3
la sedia a dondolo (lah **say**-dee-ah ah
   dohn-doh-loh), rocking chair, 2, 4
la sedia a rotelle (lah **say**-dee-ah ah
   roh-**tayl**-lay), wheelchair, 11
sedici (**say**-dee-chee), sixteen, 31
il sedile (eel say-**dee**-lay), seat, 17
il sedile del guidatore (eel say-**dee**-lay dayl
   gwee-dah-**toh**-ray), driver's seat, 14
il sedile del passeggero (eel say-**dee**-lay dayl
   pahs-sayj-**jay**-roh), passenger's seat, 14
il sedile posteriore (eel say-**dee**-lay
   poh-stay-ree-**oh**-ray), backseat, 14
il segnale (eel **say**-nyah-lay), sign, 8
la segretaria (lah say-gray-tah-**ree**-ah),
   receptionist, 13; secretary, 15
sei (**say**-ee), six, 31
la selce (lah **sayl**-chay), flint, 24
la sella (lah **sayl**-lah), saddle, 25
il semaforo (eel say-**mah**-foh-roh), traffic lights,
   8, 16
il serpente (eel sayr-**payn**-tay), snake, 20
la serratura (lah sayr-rah-**too**-rah), lock, 13
il servizio per le automobili (eel sayr-**vee**-tsee-oh
   payr lay ow- toh-**moh**-bee-lee), drive-in, 13
sessanta (says-**sahn**-tah), sixty, 31
sessantacinque (says-sahn-tah-**cheen**-kway),
   sixty-five, 31
sessantadue (says-sahn-tah-**doo**-ay), sixty-two,
   31
sessantanove (says-sahn-tah-**noh**-vay),
   sixty-nine, 31
sessantaquattro (says-sahn-tah-**kwaht**-troh),
   sixty-four, 31
sessantasei (says-sahn-tah-**say**-ee), sixty-six, 31
sessantasette (says-sahn-tah-**sayt**-tay),
   sixty-seven, 31
sessantatrè (says-sahn-tah-**tray**), sixty-three, 31
sessantotto (says-sahn-**toht**-toh), sixty-eight, 31
sessantuno (says-sahn-**too**-noh), sixty-one, 31
sesto (**say**-stoh), sixth, 31
settanta (sayt-**tahn**-tah), seventy, 31
settantacinque (sayt-tahn-tah-**cheen**-kway),
   seventy-five, 31
settantadue (sayt-tahn-tah-**doo**-ay), seventy-two,
   31
settantanove (sayt-tahn-tah-**noh**-vay),
   seventy-nine, 31
settantaquattro (sayt-tahn-tah-**kwaht**-troh),
   seventy-four, 31
settantasei (sayt-tahn-tah-**say**-ee), seventy-six, 31
settantasette (sayt-tahn-tah-**sayt**-tay),
   seventy-seven, 31
settantatrè (sayt-tahn-tah-**tray**), seventy-three,
   31
settantotto (sayt-tahn-**toht**-toh), seventy-eight, 31
settantuno (sayt-tahn-**too**-noh), seventy-one, 31
sette (**sayt**-tay), seven, 31
settimo (**sayt**-tee-moh), seventh, 31

English-Italian Glossary and Index

fence, il recinto, 9
fender, il paraurti, 14
fern, la felce, 24
field, il campo, 24
fifteen, quindici, 31
fifth, quinto, 31
fifty, cinquanta, 31
fifty-eight, cinquantotto, 31
fifty-five, cinquantacinque, 31
fifty-four, cinquantaquattro, 31
fifty-nine, cinquantanove, 31
fifty-one, cinquantuno, 31
fifty-seven, cinquantasette, 31
fifty-six, cinquantasei, 31
fifty-three, cinquantatrè, 31
fifty-two, cinquantadue, 31
file, la lima, 3
file cabinet, lo schedario, 13
film, la pellicola, 21
fin, la pinna, 22
find, trovare, 27
finger, il dito, 11
fingernail, l'unghia, 12
fire, il fuoco, 24
fire engine, l'autopompa, 16
fire escape, la scala di sicurezza, 8
fire fighter, il pompiere, 15
fire hydrant, l'idrante, 8
fire station, la stazione dei pompieri, 8
fireplace, il focolare, 2
first, primo, 31
fish, il pesce, 1, 10
fisherman, il pescatore, 15
fishhook, l'amo, 22
fishing, la pesca, 24
fishing line, la lenza, 22
five, cinque, 31
fix, aggiustare, 27
flags, le bandiere, 17
flamingo, il fenicottero, 20
flashbulb, il riflettore, 21
flashlight, la lampadina tascabile, 3
flat tire, la gomma a terra, 14
flight attendant, l'assistente di volo, 17
flint, la selce, 24
flipper, la pinna, 22
floor, il pavimento, 2
florist, la fiorista, 15
flour, la farina, 3
flowerbed, l'aiuola, 5
flowers, i fiori, 5
flute, il flauto, 19
fly (insect), la mosca, 5; (verb), volare, 27
fly swatter, il chiappamosche, 5
fog, la nebbia, 5
food, il cibo, 6
food processor, il food processor, 3
foot, il piede, 11
football (game), il football americano, 18; (ball), la palla, 18
footprint, l'orma, 23
footstool, il posapiedi, 2
forehead, la fronte, 11
foreman, il capomastro, 15
forest, la foresta, 25
forge, la fornace, 25
fork, la forchetta, 10
forty, quaranta, 31
forty-eight, quarantotto, 31
forty-five, quarantacinque, 31
forty-four, quarantaquattro, 31
forty-nine, quarantanove, 31
forty-one, quarantuno, 31
forty-seven, quarantasette, 31
forty-six, quarantasei, 31
forty-three, quarantatrè, 31
forty-two, quarantadue, 31
fountain, la fontana, 8
four, quattro, 5, 31
fourteen, quattordici, 31
fourth, quarto, 31
fox, la volpe, 20
freckles, le lentiggini, 12

freezer, il congelatore, 3
french fries, le patatine fritte, 10
French horn, il cornetto, 19
frog, la rana, 9
frozen dinner, il pranzo surgelato, 6
fruit, le frutta, 6
fruit juice, il succo, 6
full, pieno, 26
fur, la pelliccia, 24

galaxy, la galassia, 23
game, il gioco, 4
garage, il garage, 14
garden hose, l'idrante, 5
gardener, il giardiniere, 15
garment bag, il sacco per abiti, 17
gas cap, il coperchio del serbatoio, 14
gas pump, la pompa della benzina, 14
gas station, la stazione di servizio, 14
gate, la porta, 17
giant, il gigante, 25
gift, il regalo, 10
gills, le branchie, 22
giraffe, la giraffa, 20
girl, la ragazza, 9
give, dare, 27
glacier, il ghiacciaio, 32
glass, il bicchiere, 10
glasses, gli occhiali, 7
globe, il globo, 1
gloves, i guanti, 7
glue, la colla, 1
go, andare, 27
go! avanti, 16
goat, la capra, 9
goggles, gli occhiali di protezione, 18
gold (color), dorato, 28; (metal), l'oro, 22
golf, il golf, 18
golf club, la mazza da golf, 18
good, buono, 26
goose, l'oca, 9
gorilla, il gorilla, 20
gosling, il papero, 9
grandfather, il nonno, 29
grandma, la nonna, 29
grandmother, la nonna, 29
grandpa, il nonno, 29
grapefruit, il pompelmo, 6
grapes, le uva, 6
grass, l'erba, 9
grasshopper, la cavalletta, 5
gray, grigio, 28
green, verde, 28
green beans, i fagiolini, 6
grocery store, la drogheria, 8
guitar, la chitarra, 19
gulf, il golfo, 32
gym shoes, le scarpe da tennis, 7
gymnastics, la ginnastica, 18

hair, i capelli, 12
hair dryer, l'asciugacapelli, 12
hair spray, lo spruzzo, 12
hairstylist, la parrucchiera, 12
half, metà, 31
ham, il prosciutto, 10
hamburger, la svizzera, 10
hammer, il martello, 3
hammock, l'amaca, 5
hand (clock), la lancetta, 1; (person), la mano, 11
hand brake, il freno a mano, 14
handkerchief, il fazzoletto, 7
handlebars, il manubrio di bicicletta, 14
handstand, la verticale, 21
hang glider, l'aliante, 16
hangar, l'aviorimessa, 17
hanger, l'attaccapanni, 2
happy, felice, 26
hard, duro, 26
harp, l'arpa, 19
hat, il cappello, 4, 7

hay, il fieno, 9
head, la testa, 11
headlight, il fanalo, 14
headset, la cuffia, 17
headstand, la verticale sulla testa, 21
heavy, pesante, 26
helicopter, l'elicottero, 16
helm, l'elmo, 22
helmet, l'elmetto, 18
hen, la gallina, 9
high jump, il salto in alto, 18
hiking boots, gli scarponi, 7
hill, la collina, 9
hippopotamus, l'ippopotamo, 20
history, la storia, 24
hockey, l'hockey, 18
hole punch, la perforatrice per carta, 1
hood (clothing), il cappuccio, 7; (car), il cofano, 14
hoof, lo zoccolo, 20
hoop, il cerchio, 21
horns, le corna, 9, 20
horse, il cavallo, 9
horse racing, la corsa da cavalli, 18
horseback riding, l'equitazione, 18
horseshoe, il ferro di cavallo, 25
hospital, l'ospedale, 8
hot, caldo, 26
hot-air balloon, il pallone, 16
hotel, l'albergo, 8
house, la casa, 2
hubcap, il coprimozzo, 14
human history, la storia umana, 24
hump, la gobba, 20
hundred, cento, 31
hundred thousand, cento mila, 31
hunt, la caccia, 26
hunter, il cacciatore, 24
hurdles, la corsa a ostacoli, 18
hut, la capanna, 24
hypodermic needle, l'ago, 11

ice, il ghiaccio, 5
ice cream, il gelato, 10
ice cubes, i ghiacci, 3
iceberg, l'iceberg, 32
icecap, la calotta polare, 32
icicle, il ghiacciolo, 5
in front of, davanti, 26
Indian Ocean, l'Oceano Indiano, 32
ink pad, il tampone, 13
insect, l'insetto, 24
inside, indietro, 26
intersection, l'incrocio, 16
iron, il ferro da stiro, 3
ironing board, la tavola da stiro, 3
island, l'isola, 32

jack, il cricco, 14
jacket, la giacca, 7
jaguar, il giaguaro, 20
jail, il carcere, 8
jam, la marmellata, 10
jeans, i jeans, 7
jeep, il jeep, 16
jellyfish, la medusa, 22
jewel, il gioiello, 22
jeweler, il gioielliere, 15
jigsaw puzzle, il rompicapo, 4
jogging, il footing, 18
judge, il giudice, 15
juggle, fare giochi, 27
juggler, il giocoliere, 21
jump, saltare, 27
jump rope, la corda, 4
jungle, la giungla, 32
jungle gym, l'attrezzo ginnico, 8

kangaroo, il canguro, 20
ketchup, il ketchup, 10
kettle, il bollitore, 3
key, la chiave, 13

kick, dare un calcio, 27
kickstand, il cavalletto, 14
kid, il capretto, 9
kiln, la fornace, 24
king, il re, 25
kitchen, la cucina, 2, 3
kite, l'aquilone, 5
kitten, il gattino, 9
knee, il ginocchio, 11
knife, il coltello, 10
knight, il cavaliere, 25
knitting needles, i ferri da calza, 4
knot, il nodo, 13

lab coat, il camice, 23
label, l'etichetta, 13
laboratory, il laboratorio, 23
ladder, la scala a pioli, 23
lake, il lago, 32
lamb, l'agnello, 9
lamp, la lampada, 2
lance, la lancia, 25
landing capsule, la capsula spaziale, 23
landing gear, il carrello d'atterraggio, 17
large, grande, 26
laugh, ridere, 27
laundry, il bucato, 3
laundry detergent, il detersivo, 3
lawn mower, la falciatrice meccanica, 5
lawyer, l'avvocatessa, 15
leaf, la foglia, 5
leather, il cuoio, 24
left, sinistro, 26
leg, la gamba, 11
lemon, il limone, 6
leopard, il gattopardo, 20
leotard, la calzamaglia, 19
letter, la lettera, 13
letter carrier, il postino, 15
lettuce, la lattuga, 6
librarian, il bibliotecario, 15
light (color), chiaro, 26; (weight), leggero, 26
lightbulb, la lampadina, 4, 21
lighthouse, il faro, 16
lightning, il fulmine, 5
lime, il tiglio, 6
lion, il leone, 20, 21
lion tamer, il domatore dei leoni, 21
lips, le labbra, 11
lipstick, il rossetto, 12
listen (to), ascoltare, 27
living room, il salotto, 2
lizard, la lucertola, 20
lobster, l'aragosta, 22
lock, la serratura, 13
log, il ceppo, 5
long, lunghi, 12; lungo, 26
long jump, il salto in lungo, 18
look for, cercare, 27
loom, il telaio, 24
loudspeaker, l'altoparlante, 1
luggage compartment, il deposito bagagli, 17
lunar rover, la macchina lunare, 23
lunch, il pranzo, 10

magazines, le riviste, 11
magic wand, la bacchetta magica, 25
magician, il mago, 21
magnet, il magnete, 4
mail slot, il buco delle lettere, 13
mailbag, il sacco da posta, 13
mailbox, la cassetta postale, 13
make-believe, immaginato, 25
makeup, il trucco, 19
mammoth, il mammùt, 24
man, l'uomo, 9
mane, la criniera, 20
manhole cover, la bocca di accesso, 8
manicurist, la manicure, 12
map, la carta geografica, 1, 32
marbles, le palline di marmo, 4
mascara, la mascara, 12
mask, la maschera, 19, 22

master of ceremonies, il cerimoniere, 19
matches, i fiammiferi, 5
meals, i pasti, 10
meat, la carne, 6
mechanic, il meccanico, 14
medal, la medaglia, 18
medicine, la medicina, 11
medicine cabinet, l'armadietto farmaceutico, 2
medium, medio, 26
melon, il melone, 6
menu, il menù, 10
metal detector, il revelatore del metallo, 17
meteor shower, la pioggia dei meteori, 23
mice, i topi, 26
microphone, il microfono, 19
microscope, il microscopio, 23
microwave oven, il forno a microonda, 3
milk, il latte, 6
million, milione, 31
minstrel, il menestrello, 25
mirror, lo specchio, 2
mittens, i guanti a manopola, 7
moat, il fosso, 25
model, l'indossatrice, 15
mom, la mamma, 29
money, il denaro, 6
monkey, la scimmia, 20
moon, la luna, 23
moon rock, il cristallo di luna, 23
mop, la scopa di stracci, 3
mother, la madre, 29
motorboat, il motoscafo, 16
motorcycle, la motocicletta, 16
mountains, la montagna, 32
mouse, il topo, 9
mousse, il mousse, 12
mouth, la bocca, 11
movie projector, il proiettore, 4
movie theater, il cinema, 8
mud, il fango, 5
museum, il museo, 8
mushroom, il fungo, 10
music box, la scatola della musica, 4
mustache, i baffi, 12
mustard, la mostarda, 10

nail, il chiodo, 3
nail clippers, il tagliaunghie, 12
nail file, la limaiola, 12
nail polish, lo smalto, 12
napkin, il tovagliolo, 10
narrow, stretto, 26
navigator, il navigatore, 17
near, vicino, 26
nebula, la nebulosa, 23
necklace, la collana, 7
nest, il nido, 5
net, la rete, 18
new, nuovo, 26
newspaper, il giornale, 8
next to, vicino a, 26
night, la notte, 21
night table, il tavolo, 2
nine, nove, 31
nineteen, diciannove, 31
ninety, novanta, 31
ninety-eight, novantotto, 31
ninety-five, novantacinque, 31
ninety-four, novantaquattro, 31
ninety-nine, novantanove, 31
ninety-one, novantuno, 31
ninety-seven, novantasette, 31
ninety-six, novantasei, 31
ninety-three, novantatrè, 31
ninety-two, novantadue, 31
ninth, nono, 31
noodles, la pasta, 10
north, nord, 32
North America, l'America del Nord, 32
North Pole, il polo Nord, 32
northeast, nord-est, 32
northwest, nord-ovest, 32
nose, il naso, 11

notebook, il quaderno, 1
notepad, il blocco, 13
numbers, i numeri, 1, 31
nurse, l'infermiere, 11
nuts, le noci, 6

oar, il remo, 16
oasis, l'oasi, 32
ocean, l'oceano, 22
octagon, l'ottagono, 30
octopus, il polpo, 22
off, spento, 26
oil, l'olio, 14
old, vecchio, 26
omelet, la frittata, 10
on, acceso, 26
on top of, su, 26
one, uno, 31
onions, le cipolle, 6
open (adjective), aperto, 26; (verb), aprire, 27
optician, l'ottico, 15
orange (color), arancione, 28; (fruit), l'arancia, 6
orchestra, l'orchestra, 19
orchestra pit, la buca dell'orchestra, 19
ordinal numbers, i numeri ordinali, 31
ostrich, lo struzzo, 20
outside, fuori, 26
oval, l'ovale, 30
oven, il forno, 3
owl, il gufo, 20
oxygen tank, l'autorespiratore, 22

Pacific Ocean, l'Oceano Pacifico, 32
package, il pacco, 13
packing tape, il nastro d'imballaggio, 13
paint (verb), dipingere, 27; (noun), il colore, 1, 24
paintbrush, il pennello, 1
painter, il pittore, 15
pajamas, la pigiama, 7
pan, la padella, 3
panda, l'orso panda, 20
pants, i pantaloni, 7
paper, la carta, 1
paper clip, la graffa, 13
paper towels, l'asciugamani di carta, 3
parachute, il paracadute, 18
paramedic, l'assistente del medico, 15
park, il parco, 8
parking lot, il parcheggio, 8
parking meter, il parchimetro, 8
parrot, il pappagallo, 20
part, la scriminatura, 12
passenger, il passeggero, 17
passenger's seat, il sedile del passeggero, 14
passport, il passaporto, 17
patient, il paziente, 11
paw, la zampa, 20
peach, la pesca, 6
peacock, il pavone, 20
peanuts, le arachidi, 21
peas, i piselli, 6
pedal, il pedale, 14
pedicurist, la pedicure, 12
pen, la penna, 1
pencil, la matita, 1
pencil sharpener, il temperamatite, 1
penguin, il pinguino, 20
peninsula, la penisola, 32
people, la gente, 15
pepper, il pepe, 10
petal, il petalo, 5
pharmacist, la farmacista, 15
pharmacy, la farmacia, 8
phone booth, la cabina telefonica, 13
photo album, l'album di fotografie, 4
photograph, la foto, 4
photographer, il fotografo, 15
piano, il pianoforte, 19
picnic, il picnic, 9
picture, il quadro, 1
picture frame, la cornice, 4

pie, le torta, 6
pig, il maiale, 9
piggy bank, il salvadanaio, 13
piglet, il porcellino, 9
pill, la pillola, 11
pillow, il guanciale, 2
pilot, il pilota, 17
pineapple, l'ananas, 6
pink, rosa, 28
plain, la pianura, 32
planet, il pianeta, 23
plant, la pianta, 1
plate, il piatto, 10
play (a game), giocare, 27; (an instrument),
　　suonare, 27
playground, il parco giochi, 8
pliers, la pinza, 14
plumber, l'idraulico, 15
pocket, la tasca, 7
point (at), mostrare, 27
polar bear, l'orso bianco, 20
police car, la macchina da polizia, 16
police station, il posto di polizia, 8
policeman, il poliziotto, 15
policewoman, la donna poliziotto, 15
pond, lo stagno, 9
ponytail, la coda di cavallo, 12
popcorn, il popcorn, 21
porter, il facchino, 17
porthole, l'oblò, 22
post office, l'ufficio postale, 13
post-office box, la cassetta per imbucare, 13
postal worker, l'impiegato dell'ufficio postale, 13
postcard, la cartolina, 13
poster, il cartellone, 2
postmark, il timbro postale, 13
pot, il vaso, 24
potato chips, le patatine, 6
potatoes, le patate, 6
potter, il vasaio, 24
powder, la cipra, 12
prepositions, i preposizioni, 26
price, il prezzo, 6
prince, il principe, 25
princess, la principessa, 25
propeller, l'elica, 17
protractor, il goniometro, 1
pterodactyl, il pterodattilo, 24
puddle, la pozzanghera, 5
pull, tirare, 27
pupil desk, il banco, 1
puppet, il burrattino, 4
puppy, il cucciolo, 9
purple, viola, 28
purse, la borsa, 17
push, spingere, 27

queen, la regina, 25
quiver, la faretra, 25

rabbit, il coniglio, 9
race car, la macchina da corsa, 14
racket, la racchetta, 18
radar screen, lo schermo di radar, 17
radio, la radio, 2
rag, il cencio, 14
rain, la pioggia, 5
rainbow, l'arcobaleno, 5
raincoat, l'impermeabile, 7
raindrop, la goccia di pioggia, 5
rake, il rastrello, 5
raspberries, i lamponi, 6
rat, il ratto, 25
razor, il rasoio, 12
read, leggere, 27
rearview mirror, lo specchietto retrovisore, 14
receive, ricevere, 27
receptionist, la segretaria, 13
record, il disco, 2
record player, il giradischi, 2
rectangle, il rettangolo, 30

red, rossi, 12; rosso, 28
referee, l'arbitro, 18
reflectors, i riflettori, 14
refrigerator, il frigorifero, 3
reins, le briglie, 25
reporter, il cronista, 15
rest rooms, i gabinetti, 21
restaurant, il ristorante, 8, 10
return address, l'indirizzo del mittente, 13
rhinoceros, il rinoceronte, 20
rice, il riso, 10
ride a bicycle, andare a bicicletta, 27
right, destro, 26
ring (jewelry), l'anello, 7; (circus), l'arena, 21
ringmaster, il presentatore, 21
rings (planet), i circoli, 23
river, il fiume, 32
road, la strada, 9
roar, ruggire, 27
robot, il robot, 23
rock, la roccia, 24
rocket, il missile, 23
rocking chair, la sedia a dondolo, 2, 4
rocking horse, il cavallo a dondolo, 4
roller skates, i pattini a rotelle, 16
roof, il tetto, 2
rooster, il gallo, 9
rope, la corda, 19, 21
rope ladder, la scala per arrampicarsi, 21
rowboat, la barca a remi, 16
rubber band, l'elastico, 13
rubber stamp, il timbro, 13
rug, il tappeto, 1
ruler, la regola, 1
run, correre, 27
running, il correre, 18
runway, la pista, 17

saber-toothed tiger, la tigre preistorica, 24
sad, infelice, 26
saddle, la sella, 25
safe, la cassaforte, 13
safety deposit box, la cassetta di sicurezza, 13
safety net, la rete di sicurezza, 21
sail, la vela, 16
sailboat, la barca a vela, 16
sailing, l'andare a vela, 18
sailor, il marinaio, 15
salad, l'insalata, 10
salesman, il commesso, 15
saleswoman, la commessa, 15
salt, il sale, 10
sand, la sabbia, 22
sandals, i sandali, 7
sandbox, il recinto con sabbia, 8
sandpaper, la carta vetrata, 3
sandwich, il tramezzino, 10
satellite, il satellite, 23
saucer, il piattino, 10
sausages, le salsiccie, 10
saw, il saracco, 3
saxophone, il sassofono, 19
scale, la bilancia, 6, 13
scales (fish), le scaglie, 22
scarf, la sciarpa, 7
scenery, il scenario, 19
school, la scuola, 8
school (of fish), il banco, 22
school bus, l'autobus per scuola, 16
scientist, lo scienziato, 23
scissors, le forbici, 1, 12
scooter, il monopattino, 16
screw, la vite, 3
screwdriver, il cacciavite, 3
script, il copione, 19
scuba diver, il tuffatore subacqueo, 22
sea, il mare, 32
sea horse, il cavallo di mare, 22
sea turtle, la tartaruga di mare, 22
sea urchin, il riccio di mare, 22
seal, la foca, 20
seashell, la conchiglia, 22

seasons, le stagioni, 5
seat, il sedile, 17
seat belt, la cintura di sicurezza, 14
seaweed, l'alga marina, 22
second, secondo, 31
secretary, la segretaria, 15
security camera, la telecamera di sicurezza, 13
security guard, la guardia, 13
seesaw, il su in giù, 8
sell, vendere, 27
seven, sette, 31
seventeen, diciasette, 31
seventh, settimo, 31
seventy, settanta, 31
seventy-eight, settantotto, 31
seventy-five, settantacinque, 31
seventy-four, settantaquattro, 31
seventy-nine, settantanove, 31
seventy-one, settantuno, 31
seventy-seven, settantasette, 31
seventy-six, settantasei, 31
seventy-three, settantatrè, 31
seventy-two, settantadue, 31
sewing machine, la macchina per cucire, 19
shadow, l'ombra, 9
shampoo, lo shampoo, 12
shapes, le forme, 30
shark, lo squalo, 22
sharp, tagliente, 26
shaving cream, la crema da barba, 12
sheep, la pecora, 9
sheet, il lenzuolo, 2
sheet music, le carte di musica, 19
shelf, lo scaffale, 2
shield, lo scudo, 25
shipwreck, il relitto di nave naufragio, 22
shirt, la camicia, 7
shoelace, la stringa, 7
shoes, le scarpe, 7
shopping bag, il pacco per la spesa, 6
shopping cart, il carrello, 6
short (height) basso, 26; (length), corti, 12; corto,
　　26
shorts, i calzoncini corti, 7
shoulder, la spalla, 11
shovel, la pala, 5
shower, la doccia, 2
sidewalk, il marciapiede, 16
sign, il cartellino, 6; il segnale, 8
signature, la firma, 13
silver (color), argenteo, 28; (metal), l'argento, 22
sing, cantare, 27
singer, il cantante, 19
sink, l'acquaio, 3
sister, la sorella, 29
sit down, sedersi, 27
six, sei, 31
sixteen, sedici, 31
sixth, sesto, 31
sixty, sessanta, 31
sixty-eight, sessantotto, 31
sixty-five, sessantacinque, 31
sixty-four, sessantaquattro, 31
sixty-nine, sessantanove, 31
sixty-one, sessantuno, 31
sixty-seven, sessantasette, 31
sixty-six, sessantasei, 31
sixty-three, sessantatrè, 31
sixty-two, sessantadue, 31
skate, pattinare, 27
skateboard, lo skateboard, 16
skates, i pattini, 18
skating, il pattinaggio, 18
skeleton, lo scheletro, 24
ski, sciare, 27
skirt, la gonna, 7
skis, gli sci, 18
sky, il cielo, 9
skydiving, il paracadutismo, 18
skyscraper, il grattacielo, 8
sled, la slitta, 5
sleep, dormire, 27
sleeping bag, il sacco a pelo, 9

sleeve, la manica, 7
slide, la scivola, 8
sling, il bendaggio a fionda, 11
slow, lento, 26
small, piccolo, 26
smile, il sorriso, 11
smoke, il fumo, 9
smokestack, il fumaiolo, 8
snack bar, la tavola calda, 17
snake, il serpente, 20
sneeze, lo starnuto, 11
snorkel, il boccaglio, 22
snow, la neve, 5
snowball, la palotta di neve, 5
snowflake, il fiocco di neve, 5
snowman, l'uomo di neve, 5
snowmobile, il gatto delle nevi, 5
snowplow, lo spazzaneve, 5
snowstorm, il turbine di neve, 5
soap, il sapone, 6
soccer, il calcio, 18
soccer ball, la palla, 18
socks, i calzini, 7
sofa, il divano, 2
soft, morbido, 26
soft drink, la bevanda, 10
solar panel, il pannello solare, 23
solar system, il sistema solare, 23
somersault, il salto mortale, 21
son, il figlio, 29
soup, la zuppa, 10
south, sud, 32
South America, l'America del Sud, 32
South Pole, il polo Sud, 32
southeast, sud-est, 32
southwest, sud-ovest, 32
space, lo spazio, 23
space helmet, l'elmo spaziale, 23
space shuttle, la navicella spaziale, 23
space station, la stazione spaziale, 23
space suit, la tuta spaziale, 23
space walk, il passeggio nello spazio, 23
spaceship, l'astronave, 23
spatula, la spatola, 3
spear, la lancia, 24
sphere, il globo, 30
spider, il ragno, 25
spiderweb, la ragnatela, 25
spinach, gli spinaci, 6
spinning wheel, il filatoio, 4
spokes, i raggi, 14
sponge, la spugna, 3
spoon, il cucchiaio, 10
sports, sport, 18
spotlight, il fascio di luce, 19
spots, le macchie, 20
spring, la primavera, 5
sprinkler, lo spruzzatore, 5
square (park), la piazza, 8; (shape), il quadrato, 30
squid, il calamaro, 22
squire, lo scudiero, 25
stable, la stalla, 25
stage, il palcoscenico, 19
stairs, le scale, 2
stamp, il francobollo, 13
stand up, alzarsi in piedi, 27
stapler, l'aggraffatrice, 1
staples, le graffette, 1
starfish, la stella di mare, 22
stars, le stelle, 23
statue, la statua, 8
steak, la bistecca, 10
steering wheel, il volante, 14
stem, lo stelo, 5
stethoscope, lo stetoscopio, 11
stick, il bastoncino, 24
stilts, i trampoli, 21
stingray, la razza, 22
stirrup, la staffa, 25
stop! stop, 16
stop sign, lo stop, 16
stove, il fornello, 3
straight, lisci, 12

straw, la cannuccia, 10
strawberries, le fragole, 6
street, la strada, 16
string, lo spago, 4, 13
strings, la corda, 19
stripes, le striscie, 20
stroller, il passeggino, 16
student (female), l'alunna, 1; (male), l'alunno, 1
submarine, il sommergibile, 22
suds, la schiuma di sapone, 12
sugar, lo zucchero, 10
suit, il completo, 7
suitcase, la valigia, 17
summer, l'estate, 5
sun, il sole, 23
sunglasses, gli occhiali scuri, 7
sunroof, il tettino, 14
supermarket, supermercato, 6
swan, il cigno, 20
sweater, il golf, 7
sweatpants, i pantaloni della tuta, 7
sweatshirt, la maglietta sportiva, 7
swim, nuotare, 27
swimming, il nuoto, 18
swimming pool, la piscina, 18
swings, l'altalena, 8
sword, la spada, 25
swordfish, il pesce spada, 22

T-shirt, la maglietta, 7
table, la tavola, 3
table tennis, il ping-pong, 18
tablecloth, la tovaglia, 10
tail, la coda, 20
tailor, il sarto, 15
take a bath, bagnarsi, 27
talent show, la mostra dei talenti, 19
talk, parlare, 27
tall, alto, 26
tank truck, l'autocisterna, 14
tape measure, il metro a nastro, 3
taxi, il tassì, 16
taxi driver, il tassista, 15
tea, il tè, 10
teach, insegnare, 27
teacher (female), la maestra, 1; (male), il maestro, 1
teacher's desk, la cattedra, 1
teddy bear, l'orsacchiotto, 4
telephone, il telefono, 2
television, il televisore, 2
television repairer, il tecnico video, 15
teller, il cassiere, 13
ten, dieci, 31
ten thousand, dieci mila, 31
tennis, il tennis, 18
tennis racket, la racchetta, 17
tent, la tenda, 9
tent pole, l'asta della tenda, 21
tentacle, il tentacolo, 22
tenth, decimo, 31
test tube, la provetta, 23
thermometer, il termometro, 11
thin, magro, 26
think, pensare, 27
third, terzo, 31
thirteen, tredici, 31
thirty, trenta, 31
thirty-eight, trentotto, 31
thirty-five, trentacinque, 31
thirty-four, trentaquattro, 31
thirty-nine, trentanove, 31
thirty-one, trentuno, 31
thirty-seven, trentasette, 31
thirty-six, trentasei, 31
thirty-three, trentatrè, 31
thirty-two, trentadue, 31
thousand, mille, 31
three, tre, 31
throne, il trono, 25
throw, gettare, 27
thumb, il pollice, 11

ticket, il biglietto, 17
ticket agent, il bigliettaio, 17
ticket booth, la biglietteria, 21
ticket counter, lo sportello dei biglietti, 17
tickets, i biglietti, 21
tie, la cravatta, 7
tiger, la tigre, 20
tiger cub, il tigrotto, 20
tightrope, la corda tesa per funamboli, 21
tightrope walker, la funambola, 21
tights, la calzamaglia, 7
tire, la gomma, 14
toast, il crostino, 10
toaster, il tostatore, 3
toe, il dito del piede, 11
toenail, l'unghia del piede, 12
toilet, la toletta, 2
toilet paper, la carta igienica, 2
tomatoes, i pomodori, 6
tongue, la lingua, 11
toolbox, la scatola degli utensili, 3
tooth, il dente, 11
toothbrush, lo spazzolino da denti, 11
toothpaste, il dentifricio, 11
top, la cima, 26
top hat, il cappello a cilindro, 4
tour guide, la guida, 15
tow truck, il carro attrezzi, 14
towel, l'asciugamano, 2
tower, la torre, 25
toy soldiers, i piccoli soldati, 4
toy store, il negozio dei gioccattoli, 8
toys, i giocattoli, 4
tractor, il trattore, 9
traffic jam, l'intasamento, 8
traffic lights, il semaforo, 8, 16
train, il treno, 16
train station, la stazione, 8
train tracks, le rotaie, 9
training wheels, le ruote speciali, 14
transportation, il transporto, 16
trapeze, il trapezio, 21
trapeze artist, il trapezista, 21
trash, la spazzatura, 1
tray, il vassoio, 10
treasure, il tesoro, 22
treasure chest, il cassetone, 22
tree, l'albero, 9, 24
triangle, il triangolo, 30
tricycle, il triciclo, 14
trombone, il trombone, 19
trophy, il trofeo, 18
truck, il camion, 16
truck driver, il camionista, 14
trumpet, la tromba, 19
trunk (luggage) il baule, 4; (car) il portabagagli, 14; (mammoth) la proboscide, 24
tuba, la tuba, 19
tugboat, il rimorchiatore, 16
tundra, la tundra, 32
turban, il turbano, 21
turtle, la tartaruga, 20
tusk, la zanna, 24
tutu, il tutù, 19
tuxedo, l'abito nero, 4
twelve, dodici, 31
twenty, venti, 31
twenty-eight, ventotto, 31
twenty-five, venticinque, 31
twenty-four, ventiquattro, 31
twenty-nine, ventinove, 31
twenty-one, ventuno, 31
twenty-seven, ventisette, 31
twenty-six, ventisei, 31
twenty-three, ventitrè, 31
twenty-two, ventidue, 31
two, due, 31
typewriter, la macchina da scrivere, 13

umbrella, l'ombrello, 4, 7
umpire, l'arbitro, 18
uncle, lo zio, 29